THE INVISIBLE ENTREPRENEUR

FROM MENTAL HEALTH TO MINDSET

TABATHA BARRON

AUTHORED BY:
Tabatha Barron

EDITED BY:
Name of the Editor A. Powell

Printed in the United States of America
Available from Website and other retail outlets

First Printing Edition, 2021
ISBN 978-0-578-95409-7

DEDICATION

Thank you Mom for your continued support, encouragement, and the understanding that I AM Enough just as I am. Your love has been a consistentbeacon of hope in a crazy world.

— — — — — — — —

To my C-Suite Champions tribe, because of you tomorrow has hope. My prayer foryou is that you see the power in YOU and not allow anyone to define you, your journey, or your vision.

Do not give up! You got this!

You dictate your path not anyone else.

Each one, Teach one

TABLE OF CONTENTS

PREFACE

We have gathered stories from a few amazingly brave, impactful, and inspiring female entrepreneurs from many different backgrounds and experiences who genuinely chose to share their stories as a way to inspire others. Their desire is to be a beacon of light and hope in a place where struggling can seem to be the norm while understanding their personal experiences can make a difference to one person.

Many cliches that have been directed toward women can be debilitating and can disarm and distract women from being able to be used to their full potential. Cliches such as "You're too emotional" or "for a woman, you're a great negotiator" can remove women from the competition. Additionally, sayings such as "Boys will be boys" serve to excuse men from their insensitive speech and/or behavior towards women. These sayings can leave us feeling some kind of way.

The contributions women have given to so many different industries have no bounds. It is unfortunate that as much as women contribute, they are being marginalized in one way or another. But the contributions will shine a light for those coming behind us as a way to understand how far we have come and where to pick up and carry on with a new set of eyes.

Our individual experiences in life and business teach us and we have so much to learn. I have had many interactions with many people for many reasons and I remember having a conversation with a coach about the challenges I was facing in my business. I was completely irritated by him saying to me, "Let's take race and gender off the table and talk about strategy." I understand focusing on only the things we can change but, Wow! I then explained to him that was not an option for me because I did not have the option to take my race or gender off as it is my reality and my daily experience. I am all for talking strategy, but to first remove the things that I cannot control or change from the conversation does exactly to me what I believe the market does to me, uses race and gender as an excuse to not work with me, not to hire me, etc., and the one thing I am attempting to understand he did not want to talk about.

What I took from that one conversation, is that when I show up, I make them uncomfortable, and he did not like that feeling. Here is the problem, what he said plays a large part in the challenges I was experiencing in my business. Did he mean that he did not see me? No, it just meant he could not understand my struggle, so he needed to ignore or remove it instead of seeing it as another strategic opportunity. My continued experience with him let me know he did see my strengths. However, he was clueless as to how to bridge the gap from the cliches and conditioning he has been taught and experienced to how to handle my race and gender as a strategic opportunity and how I can use them to my benefit. I understand it takes a lot of effort because of built-in biases we all have. I wanted him to set aside his discomfort and talk to me about options, but how do you reconcile the cliches from your personal experience with attributes you do not personally have to experience? We are visual creatures and Forbes reports "you only have 7 seconds to make a strong first impression." (Anna Pitts, 2013) This is the reason race and gender could not be removed for me.

There are many of us that have different experiences with the same people, you are not alone, and you are important to us, so we want to share our experiences as a way for you to draw strength from other people's experiences. Ultimately, we hope to inspire, encourage, and support other women through a few of our personal stories of struggle and triumph from mental health to mindset when you read this book.

Acknowledgement

I would like to thank each one of the beautiful women who were brave enough to share their story with me and entrusting me to uplift and highlight their individual goals and journey for all of us to gather strength and inspiration. Because they believe that by doing so others would be inspired and learn from their experience. I met you each during my entrepreneur journey and I have been able to learn from you and I thank you for your continued support, kindness, tough lessons, accountability, and partnerships. To each of you, I wish you great success and happiness while achieving your goals. Thank you for your contribution:

Christie Reviere

Courtney Giles

Danielle Alysse Martin

Dorothy Wisnewski

Esther Deutsch

Gabrielle Haywood

Inez Bronner

Michele Johnson

Kim Ribich

Kristan Weisdack

NaToya Black

Ramona Carter

THE INVISIBLE ENTREPRENEUR
FROM MENTAL HEALTH TO MINDSET

CHAPTER 1

Entrepreneurship Is ...

Entrepreneurship is fun and hard. Entrepreneurship is rewarding and frustrating. All of these realities can live within the same experience, and they are very good motivators to keep your mental health in mind as you travel on this journey of freedom to choose, freedom to support whatever dream you see fit, freedom to create whatever you want. My strong recommendation is to think of your mental health as you think about oxygen, you cannot breathe without it so make sure you have plenty of it.

Our mindset allows us to know how to grow or how to stay the same. Our mental health fuels the vehicle we are using to go and if we do not take care of it, it can have a tragic end for us and anyone who needs us. Before you say, "not me!" or "I do not have this problem, nor will I ever have this as an issue." 72% of entrepreneurs are directly or indirectly affected by mental health issues compared to just 48% of non-entrepreneurs. That is according to a study by the National Institute of Mental Health. 49% of entrepreneurs deal with mental health issues directly while only 32% of others experienced them. (Dan Murray-Serter, 2020)

There is a lot of information available for us to evaluate and apply to support our visions. Due to the pandemic, freelance work is growing rapidly. According to the Global Entrepreneurship Monitor 2018/2019 Report on Women's Entrepreneurship, there are an estimated 252 million women globally who are entrepreneurs and another 153 million who own or operate small businesses. The pandemic has given many people a taste for working from home more independently and highlighted the importance of diversifying streams of income. However, research has found that self-employed women are at higher risk of mental illness due to gender obstacles and isolation. The study found that gender-based barriers not only affected female entrepreneur's mental health but also added pressure to their work and impeded their success. (Alice Broster, 2020).

While historical research has highlighted that self-employed people are at a higher risk of poor mental health, this skyrocketed when looking at the difference between women and men. (Alice Broster, 2020) It is extremely important that we protect our mental health by getting our stuff in order. Using therapists, peer groups, a supportive community to talk with and see your stuff from a different angle, are just a few ways to manage your mental health as a regular exercise but is not limited to the ones listed. You must find something that works for you. All of this is important to note in preparation for the journey ahead as you create the dream you want to have for yourself and your family. Research, plan, research some more and then do because waiting for the perfect time can delay your goals and success.

Brené Brown says: "Understanding the difference between healthy striving and perfectionism is critical to laying down the shield and picking up your life. Research shows that perfectionism hampers success. In fact, it's often the path to depression, anxiety, addiction, and life paralysis." (Dan Murray-Serter, 2020)

We all have physical and mental limits. Never apologize for being human because the last time I looked that is all of us. Understand your limits and operate within them.

CHAPTER 2

How it all begins

When I was younger, people would ask me how I was doing, I would respond "I'm invisible". That was an interesting way to answer the question. At that age, I had already become aware of the fact that even though I was in the room, I saw myself as invisible and my experiences supported my invisibility as well as the dismissive looks and various comments made when I attempted to share my thoughts or opinions. I was a pre-teen, awkward, working to figure out who I wanted to be, and the vehicle I was going to use to get there, so learning from the adults in the room, I learned if it is not what they want to hear, I would be quieted. Now that I am older and still feel invisible sometimes, I think about my experiences and wonder, was this part of the unconscious conditioning that happens for girls as they work to figure out who they want to be as women? Possibly?!? Little did I know that it would play a major part in how the rest of the world, that I am engaged with, would see me, and treat me, as invisible.

When I looked up the word "invisible" I found the following, a: incapable by nature of being seen; not perceptible by vision, b: inaccessible to view, c: not openly acknowledged or made known, d: not able to be recognized or identified. (Merriam-Webster, n.d.) This made me pause and evaluate how I have been very intentional with how I communicate with others. I have and always will take into consideration how my words may impact others negatively or positively because I never want anyone to feel judged or unheard or invisible. I am willing to listen and acknowledge their existence even if I do not agree with their viewpoint because it is theirs and it is valuable. Our individual experiences can shape how we engage with family, friends, co-workers, and with our businesses. Once I understood how my personal experiences guided my future I have had to make some adjustments.

At a young age I knew that I wanted to be a business owner, so I watched all of the shows that showed me what was needed. I followed the instructions of the gurus and business leaders. I used my employers as a way to learn, try out different options when it came to how to engage and treat employees and company culture. Each position I worked taught me the good, the bad, and the ugly which allowed me to ponder what was not readily available for me. I took notes and created business plans, marketing plans, and all plans that supported my future and the vision I had about the business I wanted. At this point, I had not landed on the company to be created but it was brewing. I looked up entrepreneur, as another way to research my future and I found this definition: one who organizes, manages, and assumes the risks of a business or enterprise. I could definitely imagine being the one who organizes, manages, and assumes the risks of a business or enterprise to support myself, my family, or others in my community. I can create a great working environment for us to thrive within. I was excited and concerned!

What is crazy about this is the reason I really needed to be an entrepreneur was to protect and regain the ability to take care of myself, especially my mental health. In my career my mental health seemed to be challenged because, I showed up prepared, willing, capable, and supportive of the company's goals. However, when it all boiled down I still was dismissed, disrespected, used as a token, and various other marginalized behaviors that supported being an invisible woman in a field that prided themselves on maintaining a specific appearance to the outside world, but behind the walls, it was a different story. I needed to create a respectful, inviting, profitable community for creative, inspiring, and impactful humans with the preservation of mental health being part of the company culture. We all deserve that environment.

When I stepped out as an entrepreneur, the behaviors I experienced in someone else's workplace showed up on my new journey. What on earth is wrong with this picture? Ahhhh, it goes back to the original statement I made when I was young "I am invisible". Now I have both definitions and many experiences, and I did not know I would start my journey and land smack in the middle of the same bad behavior I was working to leave. Why? Because the industries still have the same thought process about women and female entrepreneurs I experienced growing up and later in the workplace, coupled with unconscious conditioning.

I strongly believe when we follow someone else's blueprint we can get someone else's results. That does not always mean the positive outcome, it could mean the results do not match your vision. There are so many people that will tell you, do it this way, or do it my way but just do not do it your way. Who makes them the expert in your vision? This is the question I had to ask myself. I noticed with all of the programs I watched, the investors I spoke to, and the events I attended, they are all following a similar roadmap needed to build the foundation of any business and I fully understood that. However, I also noticed that in some cases the original vision of the entrepreneur was lost in the noise of the room for several reasons: they do not agree with your vision, they do not understand the vision, they do not see the value, and the list goes on.

We have all sat around a table to have an open conversation about what we are building, why we are building it, and how people can support us building out our vision. Unfortunately, too often we walk out of the room confused, frustrated, and questioning the communication of our vision and if it is one we should continue to follow. One of the things I have learned is that if my voice is not the one people hear in the vision and I am questioning the product or vision being explained, that means my vision has turned to someone else's vision and was taking on another life that would not be recognizable to those who knew the original vision. Hence the reason I am very cautious about taking on someone else's blueprint is because unless they can learn my vision and support me in growing it the way I see with strategic structural tweaks, then I am not interested in continuing those conversations. I have been considered not smart for not following other people, but my response is simple - Change does not come by doing what everyone else continues to do. The people who created the rules or system in which we are following for success does not need to be present for their intent to live on in what we do. If the system allows for suppression and you adopt their rules of engagement in your own business, your intent is really their intent and can be causing more invisibility for others.

Have you ever heard someone introduce you and say a bunch of things that would contradict who you are as a person and how you want to be seen? Would you just go with it? Don't we have enough companies out here that are created only to make money for their owners? I cannot count how many times I have encountered someone only looking to make the sale by any means necessary, which could also include a severe financial strain. Why would I follow these bad behaviors and do what has been challenging to overcome? I get to choose, and I choose me and my vision. I understand although the road will be a little harder, it is better to work harder to achieve MY vision than to settle and get the vision and outcome of others. There are many different ways to accomplish the same goal, we have to work outside of our comfort zone to walk the path you have chosen for you and your business.

The road less traveled can be a daunting one. When I get to a certain point and I think that I am stagnating in the process, my mom has always encouraged me to turn around and look behind me to see how far I have come. It is a little hard to do at first, but I then encourage others to do the same.

When I was younger I remember moving through the stiff hedges and noticing that I could not always see where I parted the bush for me to get through and I realized that being an entrepreneur and choosing to make a new path and potentially a new entry point can be seen as not following the beaten path. The beaten path does not always come with the luxury we want and need but it does come with insightful lessons and creative freedom. Diversity plays a part in seeing a different way of doing things and supporting those who are willing to get banged up to prove the concept, it can be accomplished by choosing to create different rules of engagement.

Disconnect your business' value and your own self-worth

There's a tendency for entrepreneurs to define themselves by the success of their business ventures - this can be unhelpful, especially for our mental health.

In difficult cases, entrepreneurs can end up spending more time on their business, trying to make things work, and neglect their friends, family, and life outside of work. Make time to practice self-love, and realize that the figures on the balance sheet don't define who you are, or what you're worth.

thisiscalmer.com

Do you think one person can make difference? Meet Romona Hodge, she lets us know it is possible and her example provides a peek into the mental health crisis!

CHAPTER 3

One person can make a difference

Saving Minds Coalition

Saving Minds Coalitions is committed to the health and wellbeing of those suffering from mental illness, homelessness, and domestic violence. By meeting individuals where they are, we can provide everything from a hot meal to a pair of work boots. We are committed to improving the quality of life, for those in need, through education, intervention, prevention, and treatment.

~Ramona Carter

I discovered I wanted to become an entrepreneur when I truly understood one person can make a difference. While working in the medical field I saw so many people in need of assistance but were lost with no direction and did not know where to turn when searching for help. I also witnessed so many people who were denied services needed because they did not meet certain criteria, financial guidelines or no one would listen to what they were saying. It was truly heartbreaking, so I decided to become the change I wanted to see. I wanted to provide a place where those in need felt like their cares and concerns were heard. I wanted them to understand they had no reason to be ashamed of their situation and they are not alone. We make every attempt to match clients with caseworkers and providers that looked like them in order to provide a safe, comfortable environment. This allows the client the ability to express their needs in a judgment-free zone. Because of the stigma associated with mental health, homelessness and domestic violence found within families and the community, it is important for those who feel hopeless and feel they have no options to know they do have options.

As an entrepreneur, I do feel invisible. When you have limited resources and contacts it can be a struggle to be seen or heard. Times have changed, great ideas and inventions are everywhere and without the right backing, you are like a grain of sand on the beach among a million grains of sand. Being an entrepreneur is just like being in the entertainment business: You must get used to hearing the word "no" and continuously sell yourself, your brand, and your product. I have used this analogy several times. I can walk up to 100 strangers and tell them I have the winning lotto numbers, out of that 100 people, 10 people may listen to the numbers, and 2 may actually play the numbers. You stay ready for those 10 and follow through with the 2 in order to build, fortune is in the follow-up.

The pandemic was a huge eye-opener for me. I used this time to self-evaluate. I have learned so much more about myself and I am thankful I had coping techniques in place. As far as my nonprofit concerned, I saw the need and where I could have been a great assistance for some, but a lot of services were not available due to funding. I see a lot of celebrities serving on boards bringing resources to programs with tons of funding already. It would be great to see them joining forces with some of the smaller agencies so we can service more people with different needs.

One of the most important lesson I have learned when it comes to mindset and entrepreneurship is you can have the best ideas and intentions, but without putting in the work and assembling the right team your business is just a dream. I have been at this for over 6 years, and this has not been an easy journey. I have had so many people make me doubt and question myself. I have seen and heard it all, "you cannot do this": "You are just a woman", "Ain't no big companies going to work with you", "You can't get any money to help poor crazy people", not to mention all the negative black woman comments. I get it and understand why some people feel the way they do, just look at our history. It is also hard to watch new companies pop up with some of the same ideas you have and blossom and it seems as if you are going nowhere. However, this is where dedication, desire, and determination step in. Only you know if you are committed enough to follow through with your plans. This is the time you surround yourself with positive like-minded individuals to help pick you up when you fall, tell you the truth no matter if it is good or bad but most of all, help keep you focused on the end result. One of the biggest issues I had was always trying to bring people with me on my journey that did not belong. This never ends well. As you engage with people it will not take long for you to see their true colors, the key is to believe and accept what you see. Out of everything mentioned the most important lesson is understanding the power in your verbiage and saying no and meaning it. You can speak life or death into your business and the word No can and will become your best friend.

By being a nonprofit, everyone has their opinion of how

your vision should be run or achieved. No one wanted to do the work but did not hesitate to criticize the logo and start-up plan. As a leader, I listened to everything that was said and then took that information to someone I knew with a nonprofit background and was not a "yes man". After listening to his opinion and honestly completing a pros and cons plan everything started to fall into place.

My advice for other entrepreneurs is self-care, self-preservation, keep an open mind, and do not be judgmental towards others. My self-care regime consists of me carving some quiet time even if it just 5 minutes where I do not think about anything. This is a must. I am a constant thinker so I need that time to decompress. I also love to read and the older I get I find I love a simple children's book. It is a quick feel-good read. Most importantly on a business note, my "no" is just that-"no". This alleviates the debate and solidifies that I mean what I say and say what I mean.

Remember it is not complicated. Keep it simple. I have been repeatedly told "Do not to overthink the room". There are only so many hours in a day and access to resources, make the most of what you have, and do not cry over what you are wishing for. Most importantly make your schedule and stick to it. Time is your most valuable asset. Do not waste it.

Navigating challenging situations are a little different for non-profits. As an entrepreneur and founder of a nonprofit, we function totally from donations so there is no profit for anyone to make. Every encounter is a negotiation, and I must convince him or her to part with their money or donate their time for a good cause.

I believe the world, as a whole, is experiencing a mental health crisis. Pre COVID studies have shown 13% of the world's population which equates to well over 800 million people are affected by mental health and or substance disorders. Here in the United States, statistics show 19% of adults are experiencing a mental illness this is an estimated 47 million Americans, of which 4.55% (Mental Health America, 2020) are experiencing a severe mental illness. These statistics do not include our children suffering from mental health issues, or the new pandemic cases. Pre COVID an estimated 1.38 million Americans attempted suicide. Studies also show our suicide rate is two and a half times higher at 48,344 (American Foundation for Suicide Prevention, 2021) than our homicide rate of 18,830. I believe before we leave this earth we all will experience some sort of mental health episode. If that time comes, I want whoever that person is to not think twice about seeking help. This is one of the reasons Saving Minds Coalition was born, to help us reach one and teach one how to recognize signs and symptoms of mental illness.

I believe that education and knowledge of available resources are just a few of the many key components that can be used to prevent a mental health crisis. Once a person is educated and the stigma surrounding mental health has been removed we can possibly bring these numbers down and help improve that person's quality of life.

The most powerful lesson I have learned is the importance of self-care. I had become so consumed with taking care of everyone else and being "Super Woman", I unknowingly began to neglect myself. I worked so hard to ensure everyone and everything had been taken care of until I completely burnt myself out and became useless to myself, my family, and my passion. I discovered no matter how well I took care of the crew, the ship could not sail without the captain which was me. I also realized without properly taking care of my own mental health, the best decisions may not always be made. I learned very quickly my decisions not only affected me but my family and my nonprofit. This is when I genuinely understood that self-care and self-preservation go hand in hand. As a woman I know we sometimes feel guilty for putting ourselves first. I had to remind myself, self-care and self-preservation is not a selfish act, in fact, it is required to properly care for anyone or anything else.

The survival of our nonprofit is dependent on donations and volunteers. So it boils down to who you know, which is a difficult spot to be in. Friends and family have not supported me the way I expected them to, or how they offered to, and that has been disappointing. The disappointment allowed me to see the kindness and support of strangers. I have received better commitment and encouragement from strangers than so-called friends. It was shocking to know strangers are larger supporters of your dream than those closest to you. I am thankful to those strangers.

If I could do anything differently I would have started this nonprofit sooner. I also would have focused more on funding instead of programs. At this time, I would be able to have more programs available.

I believe Saving Minds Coalition is needed now more than ever. There are so many newly diagnosed cases and people suffering and not receiving treatment we must help bridge the gap and get them connected with a provider regardless of their ability to pay. When we service a client, we are not just helping them we are healing families.

Mental health nugget: The only way for us to build a better road ahead is to share the story and lessons, hence reach one teach one. This is a way to pass informative information to support others because so many people have so many opinions.

"You may encounter many defeats
but you must never be defeated"
Maya Angelou

Dorothy has a different take on receiving information from so many people and she just asks one simple question, Why?

Let us peek into her story.

CHAPTER 4

Ask yourself why

Dorothy Wisnewski
COPYWRITER

I am a freelance copywriter, and I power inclusive economic impact with bold copy for awesome people. Before I became a copywriter, I was unemployed because of my chronic illness and disabilities, and I felt invisible. I knew there were others out there who had a lot to give to but were not getting the opportunities they deserved. So I built a business where I help people find their voices, claim their space, and make a bigger impact. I like to call what I do word alchemy because I use words and stories to create new possibilities for my clients.

~Dorothy Wisnewski

I never wanted to be an entrepreneur, but I eventually realized it was my last remaining option. In 2019, I trained for a new career as a copywriter. But I needed remote, part-time work, with the flexibility to prioritize my health... and nobody was looking for that kind of employee. Not for a rookie copywriter. Not pre-pandemic.

I needed to get out of my unemployed depression bubble and get back to helping people and bringing good things into the world, even if it seemed like nobody wanted what I was offering. So I went freelance, started getting clients, and kind of realized later that I'd become a business owner and entrepreneur.

I built my business after crawling out from a pit of despair, where I felt invisible, voiceless, and useless. I honestly thought I may never work again. That starting point shifted my expectations of and for myself. So I don't need to be on all the radars, just a few of the right ones. And I am where I need to be.

I am sure there are people who do not take me seriously because I am freelance, or because I do not work 60 hours a week, or because they do not think I act "professional" enough, or whatever. But I have the business and relationships I need, so I really could not care less about their superficial approval.

After several months, the stress and uncertainty of being high risk in a pandemic crushed my health for a few months, just because my illness, Myalgic encephalomyelitis /chronic fatigue syndrome (ME/CFS) messes with my body's stress response so much. I could not function well enough to write copy, so I had to take time off from client work and forget about revenue goals. I am so thankful we are a two-income household, and my family could still eat while I recovered. Since then, I have had to be more mindful than ever of my stress levels.

People who overemphasize the importance of mindset are often perpetuating unsustainable and harmful practices. I am super wary of people who always talk about mindset and vibrations and all the woo, because it is so easy to use these concepts to dismiss someone's struggles. In reality, many things are not under our control as entrepreneurs, no matter how positive a mindset we have. So while I do think it's critical to cultivate a solution-oriented growth mindset, I steer clear from the toxic positivity that's rampant in online business. If you are out there telling people it is easy to make 6 figures with no experience if you are on the right wavelength, then delivering crappy service or products, taking people's money, and posing with your Tesla for Instagram like someone I know... I call "BS".

Be patient and selective before investing in training and education. There are a lot of people in online business who over-sell and under-qualify people for their courses and memberships. They may not care if you are a good fit, as long as your money's good. There are many ways to succeed and scale, but you are the only one who will know which one works for you.

I do not get many negative comments in my business, probably because I have to be so selective about who I'll work with and spend time with. When it does happen, it is usually pretty clear that the person is making baseless assumptions that don't deserve discussion. When you get down to it, there are very few people who know enough about *my* business to be worth listening to.

It is important for people to stop saying you cannot afford to prioritize your mental health. You cannot afford NOT to. I meditate daily with the help of a guided meditation app. I have found it a gentler way to develop a practice, rather than going full-on "life is pain, just sit with it and return to the breath" approach. Sometimes I will incorporate yoga asana if I am feeling up to it. Both practices help me keep an awareness of how I am doing day to day. That is huge because for a while I totally dissociated from my body's needs in response to my (to date) incurable illness and untreatable symptoms.

I am also unapologetically protective of my emotional and cognitive energy in every decision I make, which is a habit informed by Christine Miserandino's Spoon Theory. (What is Christine Miserandino's Spoon Theory?) According to Christine, … Whether it is clients, keeping up with social media content, networking… there is a high bar to clear if you want in on my rare and precious productive hours. Some people and things just are not "spoon worthy," or I can only afford them in small doses… which takes away any and all guilt when I can't do something. And nothing personal, but burn me, and I will drop you like a hot potato.

Spoon Theory is just as helpful a lens for healthy people as it is for people with chronic illness and disabilities ("Spoonies"), even if you do not think you need it. A lot of serious health issues take years to develop, and you may not see them coming until they are staring you in the face. But you do not have to get sick to start taking better care of your energy.

When working to establish work/life balance, I will always still be working on that balance. The most important question when you think you *have* to do something is: Why? I cannot take credit for this, but apparently, I started a career in a heavily male-dominated industry. Through sheer luck, while I was unemployed I found a copywriting course created by a superb human being who is also a woman. Her training warns against all the hard-sell bro-marketing tactics and teaches how to write copy both ethically and effectively. It also included training on how to design a copywriting career that works for you, which saved my sick, disabled butt for sure. So, it was luck, but now that I am here? I am never letting a complacent old white dude with a fragile ego call my shots again.

As an introvert and an empath, I have never been comfortable with traditional business networking. It makes me feel barfy, rooms full of people spouting elevator speeches and handing out cards. Do you know the businessman sketches from The Kids in the Hall? That is how I felt about businesspeople. So there was a stroke of luck here, too: as I was starting my business, I found I could meet people online, and pick and choose which communities had a vibe I wanted to be part of. No fakery required, and no limiting myself to what my local business community is comfortable with.

Do not sacrifice your mental health to fit into what someone tells you is the "right" mindset. You're allowed to have ups and downs and come at a challenge from your own perspective. I am not over here performing a particular mindset to be accepted in the business space… I have a place because I am busy actually helping people and showing them with my actions that they can trust me with their true selves. Everything you want to do depends on taking care of your mental health FIRST. Everything. If you are struggling to keep it together, you will not be able to reach your goals, no matter how reasonable they seem. I've had to work on regularly taking an honest look at how I'm actually doing and taking time off when I need a reset… no matter what that looks like to someone else. Restarting my yoga and meditation practices has been a huge help with honing that gentle awareness.

I have been lucky enough not to need financing since I have a freelance service business with no employees and very low expenses. But I have always handled my invoicing and payments online, and that has been well worth the processing fees. I even have automated payment reminders set up, so I never have to have awkward conversations on the rare occasion that a payment is late.

CHAPTER 5

Becoming an entrepreneur

Becoming an entrepreneur comes easy for some but for me, I was scared all the time and it has not gone away and I do not think it will, I believe it keeps me focused on my original mission. People tell me all the time, get comfortable with being uncomfortable. Have you met me? I am uncomfortable all the time, believe it or not, I have learned to channel it in different ways but people who know me pick up on it. When it comes to the business side of things I can build a bridge from where you are, to where you want to be because that is one of my superpowers and I only give one of many options of any bridge I suggest. You do not have to take my suggestion or take the bridge I discover to help you get closer to your goals, and because of some of the responses I know my suggestions are not readily accepted by many because it breaks the rules of engagement many have been taught is the only way it works.

I am always the one who has questions and will ask my questions when everyone in the room is thinking it but refuse to ask. I am the one that will challenge the status quo because I want to grow and learn and I cannot learn from the position of," this is the way we have always done it". I am determined to use my skills and knowledge to create unique systems to help others get positive results. My determination sometimes appears aggressively, without feeling, and forceful but the intent is to support, build, and support those already doing a great job.

I have learned there must be clarity in your vision and learning how to build the plane as your moving is not a bad thing, it has helped me get clearer about the outcome I wanted to achieve. Sometimes clarity is not easy to accomplish because we are back to the place where everyone has an opinion and the ones with the loudest opinions have never attempted to be an entrepreneur. They have never supported the journey of entrepreneurship and in some cases do not agree with entrepreneurship, and then you are changing and growing as an entrepreneur and that is scary to them because they are not growing at the same rate you are. This is common and I had to ask myself, what have they done that makes me believe the answer they give to me is the one that is meant for me? Nothing. Ok, I store those suggestions or comments in the parking lot of my vision board. I can review it later if it makes sense to do so but for now, thank you but no thank you because this is added pressure that I do not need.

Change is not hard, the willingness to change is hard. Every day we wake up under the new sun, new sky and we have changed from one day to another without asking for permission and yet we are digging our heels into not changing. That type of inflexibility does not work with a growth mindset and challenges your mental health regularly. Any change supports the ebb and flow of life and much like a river, it will flow with or without your consent.

There are going to be many days filled with tears, frustration, and if you do not want to quit daily, please share your secret because many of us want to quit many times in one day, and that is normal. The next step after you feel like you want to give up is what allows you to challenge the concept of being invisible. You can concede to the narrative, or you can use it as fuel and write your own story and create the protagonist you want to be in spite of it all. My encouragement to you is to stay the course, you are needed, you are loved, and keep going until you find a fantastic support system that will support you as you thrive.

Growth is sometimes lonely. We almost have a feeling of remorse as we move and our friends and families do not. As a way to share, you are not alone we want to provide a few different ways to navigate the entrepreneurial journey. One of the ideas is to identify a business owner in a position you are striving to achieve and ask questions about their journey and use what is applicable to your business and then turn and be willing to support another business owner with a similar tactic. This is how we grow and learn together as collaborators and not competitors. We cannot do this alone but we can use other people's experiences to fuel our own, with kindness. One person's growth should not be another person's pain.

I remember an exercise during a leadership retreat once and I remember seeing all the negative comments we as women said to ourselves but would never say to other women. Christie reminds us to be gentle with ourselves and that includes the words we use when no one else is listening.

CHAPTER 6

Be gentle with yourself every step of the way along the journey

I am an online business manager supporting black women business owners with back office and project management support which includes setting up their client onboarding CRM automation to free them up to focus on the areas in their business that they enjoy and generates revenue.

~ Christie Reviere

For as long as I can remember I have always wanted to own a business. I think my first attempt was in 2005 or 2006 when I stepped into entrepreneurship. My initial reason was I wanted to be in business with my daddy as a way for us to spend more time together. Later on, down the road, it was because I wanted to be in charge of my schedule and have more flexibility. Now it is to create a legacy for my family and to show my 10-year-old nephew that he has more choices in life than just working hard for someone else.

Somedays I do feel invisible, and I believe it is only because I do not always get the type of reaction or responses that I am seeking and desiring when I release a product or new service. Other days I do not because I know people are watching even if they are not responding the way that I would like for them to respond. I launched my business in the middle of the pandemic as a way to help me refocus my thoughts and deal with depression. For me, it has been a great help for my mental health.

I have always been under the impression that entrepreneurship started with mindset. Mindset is the foundation for anything that one will do in this world, without the right mindset you will give up versus sticking with it. Because I believe in my abilities and skills that God has blessed me with, it fuels me and pushes me to not give up but instead make adjustments where needed and stay moving forward.

Interestingly enough, I can't say that I have experienced any negative comments, suggestions, and thoughts that others have shared with me. Those in my circle have been supportive of me and my journey, they have encouraged and celebrated me every step of the way. My advice to other entrepreneurs is that you have to first believe in your abilities and skills with all your heart, body, mind, and soul. Do your research before starting this journey, if you have others who are already on this journey asking them questions to help you get an understanding before you launch is vital. When you launch understand that you will at some point and time hear the word "no", do not let that no define you or your business. Do not take the "no" personally prepare yourself to be ready to hear the word and follow up to ask a question to gain insight related to the reason for the no. In doing this, it helps me to get up each day and move forward in business.

My self-care regime includes me take one day, usually Sunday, where I spend time doing anything that I desire that is not business related. Sunday is my fun day for spending time with my family, having a cigar and drink with my cousin, getting some extra sleep, reading a book, or just a day of doing nothing. It took me about 4 months into my current business before I set Sunday as my self-care day. It took some time to develop a balance. I maintain my balance by setting realistic monthly business goals for myself. I take a day each month to sit down and create all my content for social media, use the scheduling tools available to set up my posts, I have a flip chart with color-coded flashcards for my monthly business owner tip topics. I created pre-qualifier forms to obtain as much information from potential clients in advance to help me make the most of my time and theirs during the consultation calls. I automate as many things as I can in advance to create time for me to focus on other areas of my business.

I believe that mindset and mental health go hand in hand in creating the foundation for balance in your life. Maintaining mental health is a choice that you should choose every day in order to have balance in your life and overall health. Being mindful of my mental health helps me to adjust when it is needed to ensure that I am able to be my best for myself, my family, friends, and clients. The impact it has had on my journey is that it provided me with tools to set up boundaries for myself and others so that I am not overwhelmed.

CHAPTER 7

Making a change

    I spent many years of my life and I still find to this day, I am following those same bad behaviors, waiting for someone or something to show up even when they have proven to be consistent in not showing up. There are a lot of childhood experiences that play a large part in my journey as a business owner and when I made the connection I made the decision to acknowledge the changes that needed to be addressed and make the adjustments in order to improve the outcome. I say all of this to say, when I made the agreement with myself to no longer wait for the father that would not show up or to no longer wait for the job that gave me glowing reviews, to respect and acknowledge me as a great individual contributor and manager, nor could I wait for a man on a white horse to save me or direct me in the direction of my success, things began to change for me. Because they did not see me because I am invisible they were never going to support my growth, collection of knowledge, or contribution, to whatever we were in, I had to change my participation in that narrative. Once I made the connection and the agreement with myself I started strategizing on how I can be successful and celebrate my wins, large and small, for myself and others like myself, and that is when things started changing for the better.

I decided that using the voice I was given to say the things that were placed on my heart to say and to do what was innately given to me to do is the best course of action for me. Was it perfect? Absolutely not, but it was mine, my vision, my wins, and my direction and I did not feel that knot in my throat and the knot in my stomach while going after my goals. I choose myself because I am the only one that was given the goals to achieve and the motivation to complete. Others can contribute as long as the contribution is not destructive, and this does not mean a bunch of people that gaslight or cheer for all ideas including the bad ones. I mean the community that tells you the truth in a constructive and strong way that allows you to continue with purpose and support aiding you in finding the answer to the questions and positioning you for growth.

Talk about mental health.

The stigma around this issue is real and it's time it stops. Mental health affects everyone. One in five Americans (nearly 44 million people) struggles with mental health. That person could be your parent, best friend, spouse or even you. Yet, few people seek out the treatment they need, because of the stigma. It's time to treat mental health just like physical health and fight any shame or stigma associated with getting help.........

Excerpt from 5 Mental Health Rules For Entrepreneurs Forbes.com (Doane, 2018)

Kristan found a gap in the market that directly impacted her family. Her experience with balance is inspiring and allows you to see an option for balance to achieve your dreams.

CHAPTER 8

Balancing it all

At BehaviorWorx of Southwestern Pa, it is our mission to deliver holistic behavior services through training and consultation initiatives to bring practices and families from divided to guided.

~ Kristan Weisdack

I knew that I wanted to be an entrepreneur about 10 years ago but did not listen to that calling seriously until about a year ago. I identified a gap in service delivery that exists in the mental health system. Too few behaviorists are addressing the medical and biological variables that are affecting their clients. Through personal and professional experiences over the last 15 years, I have identified these gaps. They are related to vision issues, nutritional deficiencies, c-section birth, and imbalances in the gut and brain. It is my passion to share this knowledge with others to create positive outcomes for children and families with special needs.

I feel especially invisible as an entrepreneur, especially now because of COVID. I cannot network in person and miss human interaction. I feel invisible as I struggle to find ways for others to find my content, to find ways to connect with others and I do a lot of work behind the scenes. If there were more visibility and transparency about what goes into being an entrepreneur, I believe that others wanting to become business owners would have a clearer picture of the scope of work it takes.

Up until last March, I was offering in-person training. When COVID hit, I had to pivot to offering virtual training for my business to survive. I struggled at first, having to develop immersive, engaging content and learn the technology but it was a blessing in disguise. I can now train people from all over the world if I want to.

This has had more of a positive impact on my mental health in that I am an introverted extrovert. I enjoy staying home and engaging in creature comforts like a good book or television or spending time with my family. I also started my doctoral program last August so that has been a catch 22. It sparked my passion to continue my efforts but has added a level of stress each week to complete my normal roles as a mom, wife, developmentalist, and entrepreneur but now also a doctoral student.

The most important lesson that I have learned about entrepreneurship is that you must be transparent, maintain good relationships both internally and externally and maintain an open mindset. An example of transparency would be clearly communicating your mission, vision, intentions, and being your true self when you are helping others. It is also helpful to help lift others up and help them achieve success.

Take a good, long look at your support networks. If you do not have strong supports, get some. Find people that are where you want to be in business and network with them. Be proactive and schedule time for yourself into your workday.

When you are starting a new business, you will come up against a lot of adversity. Building a strong team and a strong network so you do not feel so alone in your journey and can talk through negativity is key. I have handled negativity from others by understanding where they are in life compared to where I want to be. If they are someone who is not in the same line of work or is struggling to maintain work, it helps put things in perspective. Why would I listen to someone who bounces from job to job about how I should change the way I do business? I have also handled negativity by regrouping with my thoughts, listening to audiobooks, and tapping into my network for positivity and guidance.

My self-care regime has become more about my mental health over the last year especially. I have become more aware of the ebb and flow of my mental health and the things I need to do to get through my day and to be a good wife and mother. I have changed my diet, have tried to move more throughout the day, and taken small breaks, away from my desk to eat lunch, play a game on my phone for a few minutes, or to watch a few minutes of my favorite TV show. As an entrepreneur, I struggle to maintain balance every day. I try to balance work/life/family and school out with daily schedules and by consistently relying on positive quotes, my network, and audiobooks that are uplifting. Sometimes I succumb to my own negativity and the weight that I feel and take a "mental health day", devoting with a half-day or full day to indulge in the things that make me happier.

I have had to learn how to be more assertive during meetings. I have started speaking up when I wanted to be paid more for a job, giving firm handshakes, and practicing my elevator pitch to non-key stakeholders so when I pitch to individuals of interest, I am ready. I have had to get out of my own damn way and convey with passion and purpose for making a difference in the world without a bit of reluctance.

You have to have a strong network of people to rely on to maintain a positive mindset and quality mental health status. Networking, building quality relationships, reading audiobooks, and mapping out ideas on paper consistently is key. Creating a vision board has been a big help as well. Do not be afraid to ask for help when you need it - you are not alone, even though it feels like it a lot of the time.

The most powerful lesson that I have learned about mental health and entrepreneurship is that you must find balance in work/life/family tasks. I found that it is also important to have a strong team - in your family, your business, and in your network. Without these things, you will feel burnt out and overwhelmed very quickly.

Where I am now?

I have hired 3 employees and have been working on growing my business on social media including Instagram, YouTube, and Facebook. I am also getting ready to go on tour. Behaving Badly: The Laugh & Learn Tour is focused on delivering practical knowledge about holistic behavior approaches and simple interventions in engaging, entertaining, and creative ways. The target audience is early intervention professionals and parents of young children.

My goal is to educate people about complex bio-medical issues that cause behavior in easy-to-understand ways. My greatest joy has been having other people believe in what I am doing and supporting me on a regular basis. That has made such a big difference - knowing other people believe in you AND showing up to prove they are there to help. When I started really putting myself out there early last year to provide trainings, I never would have imagined going on tour and speaking at large venues. I now have the team and self-confidence to put this message out to the world. I am truly grateful, humbled, and excited for what the future has in store for me and my team. We are going to help a lot of people!

Learning there is a gap is just the beginning, what you do about it is what Esther shows us in her experience.

CHAPTER 9

If you notice something that you do not like or does not exist…

 RCS PROFESSIONAL SERVICES

We help small and medium-sized businesses leverage technology to become spectacular! We do this through our Managed IT and Cybersecurity services and strategic advisory solutions.

~ Esther Deutsch

I believe that I wanted to be an entrepreneur before I even learned how to talk. I built my first resume when I was about eight years old, followed soon after by my LinkedIn profile and first Instagram account (I now have 4 others) and included work experience like "Day Camp Director" (with the help of mom of course), Fundraiser (yes, I raised thousands of dollars for an organization for victims of terror), and telecommunications expert (encompassing my years selling financial services for my dad's company. Growing up in a small town in Pennsylvania, I have always wanted to do three things: make a difference, make money, and work in corporate, and entrepreneurship seemed like the best way for me to do what I love and accomplish everything.

I have been very blessed to be surrounded mostly by terrific leaders and mentors who have believed in me and pushed me to be the best version of myself. One thing I will say is that working as a female in an all-male company has posed some challenges like not having a woman's bathroom and those have led me to realize how important my social work background has become in the corporate world. I am very social and loved being in a physical office, so even though I work in tech, the pandemic and working from home has been a huge shift for me. I am still figuring out my work-life balance and how to navigate that, but I have learned to take more breaks and set more boundaries and it has also been an awesome opportunity to broaden my community virtually. I have met so many amazing people from all over the world (specifically through my networking and development group www.inthistogetherroundtable.com) whom I am sure I would otherwise have not have gotten to know.

I am a firm believer that anyone can be a leader and that the world desperately needs more leaders. The difference between success and failure is commitment and perspective. Anyone can do anything if they only believe it is possible. One of my favorite quotes is, "Nothing is impossible. The word itself says, 'I'm possible."

I am not sure that I would do anything differently in my journey. I think I would just remind myself to enjoy the process and take every opportunity (YOLO: you only live once) and not worry about what other people say or think. Oh actually, I would tell myself to trust myself more because I already have all the answers. I just need to look deep inside myself.

My belief is that we are in this world to change it. if something does not exist, I prefer to create it (not just talk about it. I think that this is the best way to impact change and show people through action how to be different. As an entrepreneur, if you believe it, you can achieve it. Also, "Leadership is a stance in the world, not a job title." if you notice something that you do not like or does not exist, it is because it is your obligation to change or create it!

My self-care regimen is still a work-in-progress, but I often do mental health checks and as a work-a-holic force myself to take "me-time" away from work and my phone to focus on myself and my needs. I get manicures often :D, engage in "retail therapy," and maintain a strict workout routine which is a great outlet for me to increase my endorphins and spend time in solitude. I also read and meditate to reset mentally and am blessed to have a great friends circle and volunteer community for when I need social support. I also maintain strict work and home boundaries.

When I think about mental health and mindset, I think that every person needs to find a healthy balance between working for others and finding what works for them. No two people were created equal and comparing ourselves to others though easy - is never helpful. When I was 19 years old, I got Alopecia and lost almost all of my hair —-for over 2 years. Over time, I met many who experienced the same or similar. I quickly noticed that it was not the ones with the worst cases who managed best. rather, it was the ones who saw their challenges as an opportunity to speak out about it and help others who were happiest and that is what I strive for always.

As someone who likes to take care of others, I have had to work on learning that the more I give to myself first, the more I will be able to help the world. "You can't pour from an empty cup" is something I am always working to internalize. Though I work very corporate and always have been, I became a Social Worker at the age of 23 so obviously, mental health is very important to me. I embarked on a personal health journey (you can check it out on Instagram under @scalestruck a few years ago and have never looked back. It was that journey, that led me to work with "at-risk" students in a mentorship capacity.

Where am I now?

Although I am a social worker by education, I am proud to work as the General Operations Manager at a wonderful IT support company called RCS Professional Services. There are so many things I love about my work but a few of the highlights are my colleagues, our partners and all our clients who have become so much more than just "the people I work with" and am proud to call my friends and even extended family. As part of my job, I also get to run a few weekly networking groups. One of them, called "In This Together Roundtable" (www.inthistogetherroundtable.com) is the highlight of my Tuesday morning and has helped me not only grow our business but also build life-long friends.

CHAPTER 10

Community is how you make it!

Community is very important to the success of any business. As humans, we need a community to help us learn the limits and boundaries to becoming the best versions of ourselves. The community teaches the lessons, gives us examples, and provides hard knocks we will experience as we handle the triumphs needed to support each other in breaching the invisible ceiling. What I call limits the world calls failures. My take is failure is when you give up and your vision follows suit. What I took from Thomas Edison is he found

10,000 ways it didn't work but it only takes 1 way for it to work. Test and measure. Test and measure. This is how the limits are found, find them faster and change a little to find the right path for YOU!

I asked myself, who do you need in your tribe or community? This is where we find the right people and not the "yes person" or the neutral cheerleader that will not share the information needed for you to improve. I looked at my network, and I picked other female entrepreneurs that had the characteristics I admired, the learning spirit that allowed me to be creative, the energy I can draw from, and the authenticity they continue to operate with and created my inner circle and community that shows up authentically themselves with no expectations and with a willingness to support me and others with accumulated knowledge from their individual journey. The subject line read, "I choose you".

I have been implementing business practices according to other people's strong recommendations or encouragement and have not found it to be successful but when I do it my way I get the results expected because I have done the research and I understand my why and my vision. My results are not always in an effort to making the sale, it is about gaining the knowledge to add to my experience to be better prepared to sell. Community supports you when you belong to the right one. In the event you do not have access to a community that supports you in the way you need, you have the right to create it and invite people you admire, respect, and would like to learn lessons from and grow with them. I found myself in this situation and created a spectacular group of ladies because the market and the people did not have what I was looking to join. When creating the community you want to see, establishing boundaries, mutual respect, honesty, and the understanding of the group is extremely important. Protecting your circle is important to the support you will need.

There is a difference between networking and supporting. When you join or create a supportive team, you will not need to pass around your business cards. You will not need to be envious of someone else's success. You will only see how you can help someone else grow because their growth is a case study for your own growth. Your mental health and mindset will have a safe space for you to go and grow with others.

When you have community, we also have to work on finding the proper outlet to keep the stress at bay or to at least minimize it. NaToya has a great viewpoint on that subject. Let's take a look.

CHAPTER 11

Finding an outlet

Ink & Identity LLC

I am an editor and writer. As an editor, I specialize in developmental editing and copy editing. If you have written, are writing, or desire to write a book I will make the process easier for you. I help people tell their phenomenal story in a powerful way. As a writer, I specialize in writing website content. I will ink your identity.

~NaToya Black

I think on some level I have always wanted to be an entrepreneur. Even as a young adult, if there was something I felt should be happening or be done, I would simply do it myself. I was not afraid to create what I wanted to see. However, entrepreneurship is not an actual career choice, at least it was not for me. As I was the first person in my immediate family to go to college, and being the practical person I am, I went to school declaring I wanted to be a doctor. That did not last long. After a long and twisting journey, I ended up in corporate America with degrees in business. By trade, I am a Human Resources professional. However, in 2017 I started searching for a way to tap into my dormant gifts. I invested in training and coaching programs geared towards entrepreneurship. But nothing seemed right, so I continued my career path. As a matter of fact, I absolutely love my current job. It is the perfect job for me. But after about a year in the position, I realized there was still something missing. I wanted to do more and help people in a different way. Around the same time, the scripture Esther 4:14 kept popping up in my life. I knew this scripture was meant to give me the push I needed to move forward. So, I decided to create the space to help people in a way I knew could be impactful because I had personally experienced it. While going through some major life transitions, I began to journal. Writing helped me understand, accept, and appreciate my difficult journey. Writing was therapeutic for me. By writing my complete and unfiltered story, I gave myself permission and gained the strength I needed to move forward. I knew I was not the only person with an amazing story. Thus, I decided to use my gift and passion for reading and writing to help others change the narrative of their lives with their words. As a result, Ink & Identity LLC was born.

I often feel invisible as an entrepreneur. However, I will admit that some of that invisibility is due to my own actions. There is a lot of pressure to succeed when you decide to become an entrepreneur. That can be difficult because people have their own idea of what success should look like for you, so I have tried to keep my business quiet. I thought, "If I just keep it quiet and not tell many people about my business, then if I fail not too many people will know. If I fail everyone is going to see me. Everyone is going to be disappointed. I am going to be so embarrassed. People aren't just going to think I failed at my business, they're going to think I am a failure." I have never wanted to be a failure. It is one of my biggest fears. I did not want to tell people about my business. And the few people I did share my business with tried to support me the best way they could. Some people were amazing and very encouraging. Others made me feel like I just had a hobby. They could not understand the intangible things I had to do for my business. They could not understand me working on something like my business structure and core values. "Why can't you just edit somebody's book? Why do you have to do all that?" They meant well, but it made me uncomfortable. I know what they said, but I heard, "You don't know what you're doing." It made me feel like a fraud, not a real editor, not a real entrepreneur.

The pandemic forced me to be still and really self-assess. The time away from people helped me to understand who I needed close to me and those who needed to be shifted in my life. It was a positive experience because so many other voices were silenced. I could hear God. I could hear me. I had the quiet time to figure out the things that were changing in my life and truly ponder the next step God had for me. The pandemic gave me the time to acknowledge my true passions and gifts, as well as the opportunity to discover some new ones. As a result, my business was conceived and birthed during the pandemic.

Entrepreneurship has a way of bringing all your insecurities to the surface. If you have deep-rooted or even apparent feelings of inadequacy, low self- esteem, or low self-worth, it will come out when you become an entrepreneur. A big part of entrepreneurship is communicating the value of what you provide to your potential clients/customers. If you do not believe in yourself and what you have to offer, you will not be able to convince anyone else. I learned this lesson the hard way. When I first started my business, I was super excited. However, as soon as I encountered someone I thought was smarter than me, so many insecurities popped up. I had to work through those feelings in order to serve my client. It was a difficult process, but it opened my eyes to the things I needed to deal with.

The one thing that I would have done differently in the very beginning stages of my business is I would have gotten truly clear and firm on my services prior to starting. My target market would have been smaller, and my programs would have been more streamlined. I would not allow people to convince me to do things in my business that made me uncomfortable or pulled me away from my vision. I would own the fact that my entry into entrepreneurship is simply that, it is not my entry into the world or into business.

I believe entrepreneurship starts on the inside. Every decision you make will reflect your mindset and the state of your mental health. You will show up in your business the same way you show up in every other area of your life. Therefore, it is imperative for you to get clear on who you are and what you do. You need to be confident in the value you bring to the table and the gift you offer the world. Be confident in who you are, realizing that it is your authentic self that will draw the right people to you. It is also vitally important to have a good support system. You need people in your life who can lift you up on the days you feel low. You especially need someone to simply remind you how awesome you are from time to time.

One thing I recently started doing was scheduling time for myself on my calendar. I may use that time to eat a nice dinner, get a facial, or just watch TV. I do not let anyone interrupt the time I have set aside for myself. It does not matter what someone may need me to do, if I have scheduled time for me to sit and watch TV then my response is going to be, "Oh I'm sorry, I'm not available." This is huge for me because I would always put other people's needs before my own and I would always regret it; and in some cases, began to resent the person. Not making myself a priority was damaging to my mental health as well as my relationships. So, this was something that I was forced to do. I realize I need to be mentally healthy not only as an entrepreneur but as a mother and a woman who has a purpose on this earth.

I think mindset and mental health are often viewed as two separate things. However, in my personal experience, the two are intricately connected. When I was growing up, I only heard the words "mental health" when discussing someone with a disorder. The person was thought to have lost some aspect of their grasp on reality. As a result, I learned to be a little leery of people with mental health disorders…we could not predict what they would say or do. I now believe that mental health is the total picture of a person's cognitive functions, both positive and negative.

My personal definition of "mindset" is what you have "set" your mind to believe based on the information you have been exposed to. What you believe to be true can have an impact on your mental health. Fear, stress, and worry can weigh heavily on someone and impede their ability to think clearly and make good decisions. On the other hand, positivity and optimism can aid in dealing with the pressures of life.

Being an entrepreneur has forced me to pay more attention to my mental health. I treated my business like a hobby, so other people's projects or needs were always more important than mine. I noticed that most of the stressful situations in my life resulted from my inability to say no. Feeling overwhelmed, ill-prepared or ill-equipped, and unrealistic timelines/expectations stress me out. When I am stressed out and functioning on mental "fumes" I make mistakes and poor decisions. There were times when I was working on a project and knew I did not have adequate time to finish it; my body would resist. My heart would race, I would have a hard time focusing, and I would do something crazy afterward such as eating 12 cookies in one sitting. I have come to accept that I do not have an unlimited supply of mental or emotional bandwidth, and I am okay with that. I have learned to say, "I can't deal with that right now" instead of forcing myself to do something while trying to manage the stress. As an entrepreneur, you must show up in your business because what you are doing is important. I could not show up in my business the way I wanted to because I was mentally drained. And being an entrepreneur brought its own set of challenges and stressors.

I am always working on creating a more balanced life for myself. I have the tendency to fall into vacuums, and whatever I am doing I continue doing it until something new grabs my attention. This is great when I am focused and getting work done. However, it can be draining when I get so caught up working that I do not take time to rest. The thing that keeps me balanced now is working out.

A couple of years ago my children moved to Japan with their father. It was a huge change in my life, so I decided to find something to do with my extra time and the gym seemed like a good idea. I actually told my trainer that I was coming simply because I didn't want to go home to an empty house. And that is exactly what motivated me to start going, but once I got there, I found so much more than a reason not to go home. When I started working out, I found myself in a space where I could just be and focus on myself. No one had any expectations of me (other than to never quit), but they quickly noticed my strength and encouraged me to push myself. And it worked because most of the time I was too busy trying to breathe and not die to be sad. It did not take long before that whispered prayer of, "Lord don't let me die" turned into "Okay, do one more" which turned into "I'm a beast!" Lol! Ultimately the gym became my safe haven. It is one place where I do not feel like a failure; a place where I feel strong and capable. The gym represents one place where I get to be the heroine of my own story instead of standing in the shadow of the needs of those around me. For the first time in a long time, I got to put me first. And soon the strength I found in the gym started showing up in other areas of my life. No matter how much pressure I feel to accomplish something, no matter how much drama I am dealing with, no matter how much I feel like a failure, I go to the gym, and I sweat it out. Not because I am hiding from my problems, but because I know that with as much as I give to others, I must take time to recharge and refill. That is what balance means to me. As entrepreneurs, I believe we all need a place or a space where we intentionally block out the rest of the world and focus on ourselves. A time where we fully acknowledge, accept, and celebrate all of who we are while gaining the strength to emerge empowered to take up our plow and continue our work.

Where am I now?

My greatest joy on this entrepreneurial journey is being able to do something I'm passionate about, something that matters. I have been able to help my clients tell some really powerful stories. The best part of it is the healing they experience along the way. I know my clients tell me things they've never told anyone else. They trust me to help them voice their pain, sorrow, joy, and triumphs; their truth. And I am honored to be part of their healing process. I am currently in the building phase of my business. I'm very clear on what I do and how I serve others. My goal is to continue to grow as an expert in my field and expand my business.

One of the biggest lies ever repeated is, "Sticks and stones may break my bones, but words will never hurt me." Scratches and abrasion heal but the wrong words have a lasting impact on another person like hot grits or cream of wheat on the skin. It sticks and is hard to remove and continues to burn even after the last grain is removed. Meet Gabrielle as she reminds us about the power of our words.

CHAPTER 12

The Power of Words

We create and design women's fashionable and modest apparel, beginning with our premiere product, the "KneeKini", a capri- length swimsuit - designed with bold bright color patterns for women who want a little bit more coverage in the thigh/leg area, but they do not want to have to forfeit style.

~Gabrielle Haywood

I think I knew I wanted to be an entrepreneur as a child; although, I did not know what it was called at the time. I never heard the word "entrepreneur", I just knew I wanted to do something where I was able to create. I wanted to be in some form of leadership or have my own company...something like that. As a child, I would create things. I would draw and cut out paper dolls and then build little cities around the house where they would live, work and play. All throughout the den and living room, you would see these little paper dolls. They had businesses, shops, and churches. I created paper dolls that had businesses, shops, etc. Again, I created something... maybe something I aspired to be.

My mom worked from 11 pm to 7 am all my life. She also worked other jobs during the day while we were in school. When I went to school, my mom was basically just getting home, but she was home. And when I got home from school, my mom was home, but I always knew she worked. But when I had my daughter, although my mom moved in with me, I began to ask myself how this was going to work when my daughter begins school and I have to take her to the school bus. What happens when she gets off the school bus? I knew about latchkey kids, I knew they could come home by themselves, and so forth. I knew about after-school programs, but I was not comfortable with any of those options. I was comfortable with being there when she went to school and being home when she returned. I saw her off and when she came home, I greeted her just like my mom did for us.

At that time, I had some ideas for a business but wondered how I could pursue my idea and still generate income. I worked from midnight to eight in the morning at a microfiche company just so that I could be home with my daughter and see her off to school. When I would see various athletes on television being interviewed in some form or another, I would think, this is a kid from the neighborhood, and he may not be as polished with his communication or interview skills as he could be. I had a passion to help. With a degree in speech, I wanted to assist in helping athletes with their public image. I was very passionate about helping them polish their image. It was at this point that I started an image consulting business where I consulted with clients on voice, articulation, interview skills, media, and public image. I soon discovered the very clientele I wanted to help did not want the help I was offering. Most of my clients were either attorneys or salesmen who wanted to polish their public image; This was not the market that I wanted to serve. That began my journey as an entrepreneur. That was the early 90's, back then no one was called an entrepreneur- at least not in my circles. So I was just out there, the little Lone Ranger by myself. But that is when I knew entrepreneurship was something I had to continue in order to be home with my daughter and pursue things that inspired me creatively. I also wanted to put my gifts and talents into something I was passionate about, something that made me want to get up in the morning. I did not want just a paycheck, a nine to five, and then retire in 40 years, get a gold watch. I knew I had to pave my own way.

I did not necessarily feel invisible, not until the question was posed to me, did I understand what that might look like in terms of my entrepreneurial journey? When I started my entrepreneurial journey, I was just passionate about something, and I turned it into a business. On the flip side of that, I also turned it into a business because I thought I could pave my own way in order to be home with my daughter and still generate income. During that time, I did feel invisible. I was in my twenties when I started my first business, and because at that time no one was doing what I was doing, no one understood what I was doing, and even family members did not think I was doing anything.

One day, I remember seeing a piece of paper my daughter had written about what my mom did for a living before she retired. She also wrote what my brother did for a living, and I think she had somebody else - but she did not have me listed anywhere. Seeing that, for some reason, kind of stung in a way I cannot really explain or describe. She was a child, and her perception was her little reality. But for a young mom, seeing that made me feel like what I did was not significant enough, I thought what I did was not important, or it was not valid, or no one recognized the sacrifice I was making. I would consider that invisible because no matter what I did, it appeared like I was insignificant. My mom had a career, my brother worked for General Motors, but for me, nobody knew what I did. My mom was my biggest cheerleader, she encouraged me. I had my mom's support, but my mom did not really understand what I was doing. I worked at night for the income, but during the day, I worked in my business seeing clients.

Fast forward to the sophomore business I started. I did not feel invisible. But I also did not know the foundational aspects of business. I was asked to write a stage play by one of the elders of an outreach ministry. This particular elder was an avid believer in entrepreneurship and encouraged us to pursue that path. After I wrote the first play, I then turned it into my entrepreneurial path. Again, I was extremely passionate about theatre and had a double minor in theatre and writing - so off I went into this venture. I started doing plays all over and I did the work but I did not lay the foundation for a business. Yes, I incorporated the business, got a business license and EIN, etc. However, it was not a good foundation for the business. As a creative, I was so focused on creating that I did not necessarily focus on building the business as much as I focused on creating quality material.

Over the course of the years, being in business for myself, I think I felt invisible because I know the behind the scenes; the sleepless nights, the blood, sweat, and tears, and the effort that I am putting forth towards my idea, but nobody sees behind the curtain. When people do not see the day-to-day behind the scenes or the tangible outcome they may expect- they may take your time for granted. Some may think you are available to do anything you want during the day but in actuality, not realizing you have deadlines, commitments, and tons of work to do and you're the only one to do it, this is a misconception. When you have a nine to five, people will say things like, "When do you get off work" or "When do you get home" but not so much when you are the entrepreneur. They do not say "When are you done working" or "When will you get off", that can make one feel invisible if you allow it to. You have to set boundaries for yourself and others. The amount of work, tenacity, and perseverance that it takes, that may be the invisible part.

As a business owner, as an entrepreneur, you work more hours than you did for someone else. For me, I may wake up at 2 am with a fabric idea or a design, or an email I forgot to return. Often, I may realize someone is still in the office on the west coast or its business hours in other parts of the world, so I get up and start working. It is not like when you close your office door and you go home, you may or may not take your business home with you. Owning your own business is a grave responsibility and you are accountable to yourself and those who work with you. Nobody knows the days where you eat a salad at six o'clock and think it is lunchtime when lunchtime was over hours ago. I feel like being an entrepreneur is 24/7 as your brain does not seem to shut down, at least mine does not.

The days I get discouraged, the days I get exhausted and tired and do not want to go anymore, I feel invisible like I am in this space by myself. I have a very supportive husband, supportive friends, and family, but it is still me putting in the work and I feel invisible to the world because nobody knows the sacrifice. When your business becomes successful, people are like, "Oh my God", that was an overnight success, they do not know it was 10, 15, or 20 years in the making. As I am working diligently to better my life, to better other people's lives, and to better my family's life - it may feel like I am invisible because people do not see the behind the scenes.

The pandemic has affected me in terms of my mental health in a good way. It caused me to go deeper within myself. It caused me to get a better understanding of where I am in this season of my life, but also to be more aware and more present with who I am today, as opposed to who I was in 2018, or who

I was in 2019. 2020 afforded me the opportunity to look within and it also afforded me the opportunity to be my authentic self when it came to my mental health. A lot of times in our communities, there is a stigma attached to mental health. But there are so many facets of mental health that we do not even understand. When I began to ask myself questions it caused me to go introspective to find out who I am and how I want to show up for MYSELF. What am I doing here? What do I want to contribute to society? What matters to me? What is my core value system within myself, not just within my company? I began to acknowledge some inner thoughts, inner feelings that may have never been addressed, ones that have laid dormant for many years. I have also had to deal with my mental health from a chronic physical pain standpoint. It has been difficult to manage my mental health along with my physical health because they work together. I have had to selfishly focus on getting myself better and that means my mental health along with my physical well-being. So, the pandemic forced me to take care of myself and come out a better person, a better mother, a better wife, a better friend, and a better entrepreneur. My faith in God has been my constant rock. I feel like I am coming out of the pandemic better.

I believe the most important lesson for me, in terms of my mindset and pursuing entrepreneurship is to be mindful of the chatter in your head. I believe you have to be transparent and vulnerable enough to know when to seek help with it, if you can't handle it yourself. I believe in God, I believe in the word of God and the word of God says, I have a sound mind. But in that same verse of scripture, it says, God has not given you the spirit of fear, but of love, power, and a sound mind. I often wonder, why is fear, love, and a sound mind in one verse of scripture, but when fear comes, love moves. Within a "sound mind", you have the ability and are equipped to shut out the clutter or the chatter throughout this entrepreneurial journey.

To work on my mindset, I have to encourage myself, I have to speak life to myself, I have to build myself up in my faith, I have to make sure my mind is healthy, and sometimes that is not an easy task. I make it a point to fill my mind with education and information that is conducive to creating a healthy environment for the journey that I am on right now. I must take care of my mindset, just like you would do your physical body and your physical health. The mind is a powerful thing. I have learned how to be better equipped to handle how I react because I have made it a point to have a healthier mindset.

Of course, I have been told negative things before. I have had people discourage me from starting a business, I have had people tell me you cannot do what you want in a man's world, or you will never make it, etc. Those comments are pretty common when you set out to achieve something. Naysayers are a part of the process. I am familiar with it, and it is a part of the journey. But there were two instances that hit me a little differently. I believe it is because of the stage of life I am in and what I am trying to accomplish before I leave here, so to speak. In the first scenario I had just come up with the idea for a swimsuit and I was a little green in this industry. But I was not green in the area of starting a business and knew that I wanted to lay a good foundation for this particular venture. So, I set out to educate myself through business classes, I went to trade shows, I studied the swimwear industry, and I did the research. I tried to learn everything I could about the different fabrics and how manufacturing works in the states and abroad.

In this particular business class, we were assigned advisors. My advisor, I believe, had a product on the market and she owned a store. So she was considered a good fit for me and I was excited to work with her. I had only been in Pittsburgh, maybe a year at the time and here I am starting this business. The class was about 12 weeks, designed to give you all the nuts and bolts of a startup. In our initial meeting, the advisor said to me, "Why don't you just stick to theatre"? And "Why don't you just stick to theatre production", "I know some theater people I can introduce you to", I appreciated her willingness to introduce me to people in the theatre industry but declined the introduction because I was designing a swimwear line. I told her, I am designing this swimwear line because I believe it is needed in the marketplace. Well, she responded, let me explain something to you. Do you think you can compete with the big swimwear brands? Do you have the money to start this business? Do you have any money? How can you start a swimwear line? You cannot compete with the big swimwear companies? I listened and respectfully said, "Thank you for giving me a reality check". I appreciated her input as one who had developed a product and knew what was involved and the difficulty I may encounter. It was at that point, I said to myself, "I do not know how I am going to do it, but I am going to do it. And that is how I handled that. I fully understood what she was doing. She was trying to give me the pros and cons. She was trying to give me the reality of trying to start a business in an area or industry I was not familiar with. She was trying to make sure I was fully aware of the cost of such a task. She gave me what she had, and I chose to move forward.

The next instance came years later, as I am still in the developmental stage of the swimwear line. I was in a program with other entrepreneurs, where again I had an advisor. This time I knew the advisor and knew she had my best interest at heart and wanted me to succeed and was vested in helping me get there. We met weekly and I valued her input and her expertise. During that time, what people did not know was that I had been experiencing excruciating pain on a daily basis. When I say daily - it does not shut down, I wake up with pain, I go to bed with pain, and it is hard for me to function some days physically and mentally. This also included a decrease in my energy levels. On this particular day, I had been up all night with pain and was still trying to complete some work that was on my plate. I had not had any sleep and was absolutely exhausted. Because of some of the health issues I struggle with, while most people use electronic or digital devices for everything; I actually have to write things down in order to retain information. I realize that may be the dinosaur method, but I write things in a notebook, so my brain retains and recalls the information better. I use digital platforms in addition to writing it down, however, others looking on, believe that to be antiquated and inefficient, not knowing the reasoning behind it. It works for me at this stage of my life.

This particular day was already a difficult one and I think I didn't have something prepared as my advisor suggested, I can't recall. But I do recall what she said. She asked me "What is wrong with you?", "What's the matter with you?", "You were supposed to have xyz". "I feel like I failed you ", she stated. I am a grown woman who has gone through a lot in my life but for the first time in my adult life, I heard:

What is wrong with you?, Gabrielle, something is wrong with you. You are inadequate, you are not up to par. In the midst of what I was dealing with, I briefly let those words ring in my head, "What is wrong with you?". Those words really hit differently at different stages of life. I knew she wanted the best for me and was only trying to get to the root of what could possibly be going on with me. I understood that. But it did not make the sting of those words any less penetrating. We later had another meeting that included one of my other advisors. At that meeting, I was determined to be transparent, I was determined to be vulnerable, and I was determined to share what was really going on with me. Something they knew nothing about, nor did I have to tell them. But I felt compelled to share some insight about her words and when you ask someone, what is the matter with you?

When I sat down with them, I pulled out my notebook and my tablet. I said you said you feel like you are failing me, or I have not progressed. I explained, I have done the work, and these are my goals. Although you are advising me, these are MY goals, so for me, I am hitting all MY goals. But in terms of what is wrong with me? I deal with pain on a level every single day that the average person might need a morphine drip to handle. I deal with things behind closed doors that I do not need to share with you nor do I want to share with you but at this stage in my business I need to share with you. When you ask someone what is wrong with them, you are hitting somewhere where you have no idea of the damage you can cause. So let me explain to you what is wrong with me. I deal with pain every day, and every day I am still pressing my way through, I still show up every day. I am still laughing. I am still encouraging other business owners, and I am still accomplishing my goals, in the midst of my physical challenges and I am showing up every day for myself. I am doing the best I can with what I have before me, and I am getting it done according to my schedule and not anyone else's. During this meeting, I had to be vulnerable, transparent and take off my "Superwoman" cape for a minute. In front of these women that knew nothing about what was going on with me. Most people would think, "Oh she's too sensitive" or "she's too emotional" but I knew I had to be vulnerable. Sharing something quite personal in a business environment where we are taught not to show emotions or shed tears. I was in a space that I did not want to ever have to share the depths of what I deal with but at the same time, I felt it necessary at this juncture. As a black woman over fifty, it may have been a little uncomfortable, but I was determined to walk in authenticity. I was vulnerable, and I was extremely transparent. That took a lot for me to do! She suggested I quit because starting a business is already stressful and it is probably causing more stress on your body, she stated. She was absolutely right, but quitting was not an option for me. So I continue to press on.

That was a critical point in my entrepreneurial journey because it was like a knife somebody stuck in me using words. We are taught to be strong. In business, we are taught not to cry in public. We are not supposed to show emotions in business. I now had to show emotions and I had to show my vulnerability in a space that I did not want anybody to know the depths of what I was struggling with. I wanted everybody to look at me like everybody else. I am okay. Everything is great. But guess what? It was not! I wished with all my heart I could have kept it a secret. I wished I could have handled it as Chadwick Boseman did with his illness, he chose not to let the public know that he had a serious medical condition. But I chose to share, not for pity, sympathy, or even empathy but for the mere fact, you never know what someone is dealing with, you do not know their personal struggles, and you do not know what is going on behind closed doors, all while they are trying to make things happen.

I am pretty tough, and I thank God that he has given me strength for this journey and the tenacity to keep going in spite of my personal challenges. I was blessed with excellent advisors on this journey and their advice and input was priceless. I am so thankful for all they have poured into me, and the genuine help given to me. I know this particular advisor is one of my biggest advocates, so I appreciated everything she imparted into my development. That is why it is important to remember words are powerful and we have to be mindful of how we use our words. "What is the matter with you", implies that something is wrong with you. So, the next time you ask somebody, what is wrong with them? Prayerfully, we will think before we injure another person with our words.

That experience made me reflect on times when, as a parent, I said those very words to my child. I had to check myself because that is not okay. I have to apologize to my daughter because as a frustrated parent I have said what's the matter with you? Why did you do that? What is wrong with you? And in terms of speaking life into those words, I can only imagine what those words do to a child. Because what it did to me as a grown woman, did not sound right and definitely not okay. I know she did not mean it the way it came across, but at this stage in my life, that did not sit well. She had no idea how that hit a person that had not slept, a person sitting there with red teary eyes because of the excruciating pain I was in.

My self-care regimen is lacking right now. I practice quieting myself over the past year because of the pandemic, some of the things that may help with my mental health or self-care include hanging with my girlfriends, or acupuncture, or water aerobics, or even going to an infrared sauna, all activities we have not been able to do this past year. I love reading. I like being in a dark room and playing my music and not feeling like, oh my God, I am not being productive. Since the pandemic, I started watching silly little shows, like family shows or mysteries. Like Leave it to Beaver, Perry Mason, things that are very nostalgic that have a moral at the end, or a show where I have to figure out "Who Dun It", which are my favorites. Someone asked me recently, "What are some of your guilty pleasures?" I said Leave it to Beaver, as silly and a little embarrassing as that might sound. I watched Leave it to Beaver during the elections and during all the negative news that was taking over the airways. All of those little simple shows gave me a sense of nostalgia and a nice break from reality. Most importantly, I learned to live in the moment.

I personally challenge the concept that we all throw around, work/life balance. I read the definition of balance, it means an even distribution of weight, enabling someone or something to remain upright and steady, a condition in which different elements are equal, or in the correct proportions. So for me, balance means you are able to keep something in a steady position so it does not fall. I like to use the example of the seesaw. When we were on a seesaw, it was fun to be on the end where you are sitting down and holding the other person in the air with their feet dangling. Eventually, that person in the air wants to come down, but when you come down on a seesaw and you are both level and you are trying to steady the two of you, but someone is still moving, still going a little higher and someone is still going a little lower.

I have learned to go back to the scriptures when it comes to balance. According to Matthew 6:33 "Seek ye first the kingdom of God and His righteousness and all these things will be added unto you". In the previous scripture, it talks about food, shelter, and clothing, understanding the context is very helpful. When I think of balance, I think of making sure the priorities in my life are in order, like putting God first, my husband, my daughter, and my kids, and in doing so I make sure I am giving as much effort, communication, love, and support in terms of balance that I'm giving to this business venture.

Balancing for me means making sure you are not putting so much emphasis on your entrepreneurial journey, or your business that you are neglecting other things in your life and that means neglecting myself. I try to use that type of balance instead of saying work/life balance, because this journey is 24/7, and your relationships including your family is 24/7. So in terms of balancing, I am not sitting on that seesaw trying to balance them out, because when you are balancing like that it is all equal. Do I mess up sometimes? Do I kind of get my priorities out of order? All the time, because I am human, but it is what I do once I notice them needing to be adjusted.

I think mindset is a set of attitudes and when I decided that I had to be my authentic self, I also was okay with being a little different. Maybe I am a misfit because oftentimes I feel like I do not fit. I had to develop an attitude within myself that consisted of my values, my morals, and determining what type of legacy I wanted to leave when I am gone. As for my mindset, I try to make sure, based on some real-life experiences, that my attitude about myself is healthy. We question ourselves and we beat ourselves up, and we speak harshly to ourselves. I have purposed in my heart in this season of my life to make sure my mindset and my attitude about myself is healthy, and I do that through affirmations, through prayer, through self-talk, etc. It needs to be a healthy conversation with what you say to yourself. When it comes to mental health, you want to make sure your mind is healthy. As we take care of our physical bodies, we must ensure that we are taking as much care of our minds. Interestingly enough, I always use our cars as an analogy to discuss how we take care of our bodies. We put premium gas in our cars, we put the best oil in our cars, we get the best mechanics and specialists to take care of our cars –

but when it comes to our bodies and our health, we put any junk in it, expecting it to operate efficiently and to operate forever and that includes our minds.

So when it comes to maintaining my mental health, I have to take that same stance as I do my car, and make sure my mental health is premium. I do this by maintaining my mental health through reading the word of God, quieting my mind, and incorporating help outside of my specific circle. In corporate America or any job for that matter when you get the job, they say you have personal days, seldom mentioning mental health days. A personal day can mean going to the beach, but a mental health day is just that, care for your mental health needs and that is different for me than a sick day. I need to manage my mental health in terms of what is going on in my surroundings, what is going on within me that is causing me emotional distress. It is taboo in some cultures and some communities if you need mental health support but if you need physical therapy you get it. I am a firm believer, if you need therapy you need to get it and use whatever tools necessary so that your mental health is in harmony with your wellbeing.

I think the most powerful lesson that I have learned on this journey of being a small business owner is laying the proper foundation for your business. This will help support your mental health later on the journey, by just not having to stress about whether your business will withstand the storms business will bring. Sometimes entrepreneurship can be a very lonely road, sometimes you can feel inadequate, sometimes you can feel the biggest frustrations, and sometimes you feel very accomplished that is in any business or any job. That is why it is crucial to lay a good foundation for the days ahead.

I made a comment on Facebook one day, "I think there needs to be a counselor or a psychiatrist, or psychologist or therapist specifically for entrepreneurs". The reason I made that statement and many others agreed, is because entrepreneurs are a different breed. I have to make sure I am covered when it comes to my mental health, because some days I feel crazy, some days I feel like I am not going to make it and some days I feel like woohoo, because I am on this rollercoaster ride, and everybody is watching. Do not get me wrong, there is a lot of joy in riding this rollercoaster. But I have to say as much fun as I am having on the roller coaster - I am scared, I am afraid, and my stomach hurts. I have learned that you need to make sure you are okay. You feel like you have the weight of the world on your shoulders, you feel like nobody else is experiencing some of these emotions, and nobody else understands, that is so untrue. There are many people that have been where I am, and there are many people that have failed and many that have succeeded. You need to make sure you have the tools, you have the resources, and you have the support systems necessary to carry you on days when you are feeling out of sorts, on days when you are feeling like I cannot go any further. I have learned a hard lesson; I have to take care of my mental health.

As an entrepreneur I am going to incorporate a mental health day for my employees, everyone needs to regroup. If I can put premium gas in my car, I can put premium care into my mental health. That is my philosophy period, take care of your mental health, take care of your wellbeing.

My experiences have taught me a few things, one thing is, lay a good foundation, understand the legal aspects and implications for your business. Do your research, do not just step out there. I am an avid believer in everything you do, even if you are scared, I believe in doing it afraid - just keep moving but do your research, find out about your market, educate yourself in your chosen industry, and most importantly make sure your ethics and your values for your company or for your particular venture are intact. You must develop solid ethics and value statements for your business be it is the most aspect of starting a business. As you grow, you will have to periodically evaluate what your core value system is: what you stand for, what you believe, and how you want to convey that to the world.

One thing I think is important and worth noting: Pour into your children. When my daughter was young, she was, and still is, extremely gifted, creative, and very talented. She would make the cutest jewelry out of safety pins. She made little outfits out of nothing. She could do her own hair starting at ten years old. She made the most beautiful, handwritten greeting cards that would probably have given Hallmark a run for their money. I always encouraged her to use her God-given talents in entrepreneurship even as a child. In terms of entrepreneurship, sometimes as parents we help cultivate our children in specific areas in order to go to high school, then college, and then get a "good" job. I taught my daughter to create jobs, to be a creator, just like our Creator. We often label kids incorrectly and inadvertently, suppressing their God-given gifts. I am an avid believer that cultivating your children's gifts can lead them in the direction that they were purposed to do.

When my daughter was younger, she wanted "designer" this and "designer" that and I would always say to her put your own name on your clothes. So one day, that is exactly what she did. She got some jewels and she put her own name on the back of her jeans. She made a little jean skirt and put her own little jewels on her own jeans and what happened when she went to school, "Oh I want that, I want one", is what she heard from some of her classmates. It was important for her to see for herself what is valued by others. What an Innovator she was. I explained to her, you have that same value as designers, if not more. Although she still wanted designer clothes and there is nothing wrong with that, I taught her "You be the designer"; "You put your name on a perfume bottle"; "You put your name on an app"; "You put your seal on something".

Being an entrepreneur is one of my greatest joys. It has taught me so much and afforded me the opportunity to create my way on this journey called life. I believe no matter how hard and how difficult it might be at times; it is truly what I am called to do. When I feel otherwise, is when I will quit, but until then, I am blessed to be following a path that I had to create for myself. Is it easy? Definitely not! Is it worth it? Definitely so. It is such an exhilarating high as a Playwright to see words on a page come to life on stage, there is nothing like that experience is what I thought until I saw my first swimwear design come to life from a sketch I made.

I want to encourage readers: Whatever God has placed in you to do, be about doing that, and do not be ashamed. If you bake cookies, bake cookies, if you bake cakes, bake cakes or if you tie knots in shoestrings, I do not care, whatever you do, do it to the glory of God. Do it passionately, because somebody out there needs what you have, and people are waiting for you to show up. Your gifts and talents are God's gift to you and how you use your gifts and talents is your gift to others.

Where am I now?

After years of R&D and learning the Manufacturing process, I believe we are finally ready to launch our premier product, the KneeKini.

I have two greatest joys during this leg of Entrepreneurship. The first one for me has been - hearing women's stories as to why they are excited about the KneeKini swimwear line coming to the marketplace. Women have shared so many personal stories with me about the need for a product like this. Those stories have helped me to continue moving forward on days when I wanted to quit.

The second joy that has literally given me life, so to speak, is seeing my design come to life. The biggest joy has been knowing all the blood, sweat and tears going on behind the scenes and then to see my sketches on a sample. Seeing my designs printed on fabric and then seeing the finished product packaged. I have experienced this with my stage plays as well. When you are alone in a room writing a story and then to see actors bring your words to life on stage...that is one of the greatest blessings and biggest joys a writer can experience. And God has blessed me again to see something in my heart come to life in the form of the KneeKini Swimwear Line.

The entrepreneurial journey in itself brings me joy in knowing I am carving my own path and ultimately fulfilling my purpose in the earth.

Mental Health Nugget:

Proverbs 18:21 Death and life are in the power of the tongue: and they that love it shall eat the fruit thereof. *KJV*

It is important how we speak to others, but it is more important how we speak to ourselves.

We just learned how words impact people and now we can meet Danielle as she shares with us how negative words can be fuel for your journey.

CHAPTER 13

Finding strength in the negative

I am a one-stop shop for authors and writers who wish to self-publish.

~Danielle Martin

I do not think I knew I always wanted to be an entrepreneur per se. However, I did always know that one day I would be using my creativity to make money and impact the world. I had ideas of how I would do that but was never quite certain which route I would take. It actually wasn't until I was let go from a third job that I realized I had "money sitting in my file cabinet." I had so many poems and unfinished novels sitting in a file cabinet collecting dust. I decided to publish my poems and use my gift of words to provide a supplemental income for me and my family. That's not at all the whole story; it is, however, how my entrepreneurial journey started.

I do not necessarily feel invisible as an entrepreneur. If there is any invisibility that I feel is because of me. Entrepreneurship is being spotlighted at every turn. More and more people are pushing to support those who are in business for themselves. Now is the time to maximize my efforts and put myself in the growing spotlight. But I do not always maximize. So again, if there is any invisibility that I feel, it is because of my procrastination and lack of consistency.

The pandemic affected me both negatively and positively. I am an empath, so I mourned with the world as people continued to become infected and die. I spent many days scouring the headlines and watching the news as things got progressively worse. To say that I was sad would be an understatement. I was devastated and overwhelmed. Eventually, after all the loss and the fact that any day could be my last, I started living with more intention. I realized that if I had passed away, I would not have reached my full potential. I realized that I had so much more to offer to the world. There is this quote I love and have been quoting since I was a little girl: "Get busy living or get busy dying." That is from *The Shawshank Redemption*. The pandemic made me realize that I had not been busy living, and I wanted to live. So, while the pandemic was awful and scary and took the entire world by storm, it also caused a lot of us to take inventory… to change our perspective on a lot of things… and more importantly, to value our own lives. I did not do much business last year because of everything that was going on, but I did begin to work on the areas in my personal life that would help me to do business better.

Be absolutely clear about what you desire of your business and your ideal client. Those are things that you cannot leave to chance. All money is not good money. And although we are all in this because of our passions, we also want to make money. Do not operate from a place of lack just because you want to make money. If your mindset is all over the place, you will attract "all over the place" clients, customers, or businesses. If you know who you are, are confident about what value you add to your client/customer's life, and have a clear vision for your business, you will attract the like.

If there is one thing I would do differently, it would be to not operate from a place of lack. That is a huge mistake that I made over and over again. I needed the money, so I took the business; I needed the money, so I discounted my prices; I needed the money, so I bit off more than I could chew. I did not realize until I was years in my business how I was hurting myself and my clients by operating from a place of lack. When we operate from any of our insecurities or fears, we are ultimately not serving ourselves or the people we have been called to serve.

I am different when it comes to negative comments from others. This is where my disdain for people telling me what to do comes into play. I rarely internalize negative comments and suggestions. I have always believed that every person and situation is different, and I do not allow others to push their thoughts and experiences onto me. An example I would like to give is when I was on my first corporate job. I had moved up pretty quickly in the company. The third position from the top in the department I was working in became available, and I wanted it. All of my African-American co-workers told me I shouldn't waste my time applying. I was told that in all the years the company had existed, they had never hired a person of color for that position. In fact, all of them had applied at some point or another and were passed over. Little did they know; I was more motivated by their negative talk. I knew the value I brought to that company. I also did not care anything about what had not been done before. I refused to take on their experience as my own and applied anyway. And guess what! You already know. I got the position. Youngest to ever get it and the first black person to ever get it. I operate this same way in my business. I hear negative talk all the time and how much of a dreamer I am and how I would never become a millionaire doing what I do. It makes me laugh. I am really not the person you can tell something won't work or what shouldn't be done. I encourage anyone else to not be that kind of person either. Each person is unique; each situation is unique. If we never did things because of what someone thought or said, well, then we would never do anything.

I think mindset and mental health are extremely important. I believe they are the foundation for our lives, be it rocky or solid. The better shape you are in mentally, the better you show up for yourself and others. I am a huge proponent of being aware of your thoughts, challenging those thoughts, and taking control of your thoughts. Proverbs 23:7 says, "For as he thinketh in his heart, so is he…" I have learned how true this is on the positive side and the negative side.

The most powerful lesson I have learned about mental health and entrepreneurship is that it is important for you to know your worth and that you are valuable. This is important because if you do not, you will accept anything from clients, you will undersell your products and services, and you will not operate your business at an optimal level. My prices as a beginner were actually too low now that I have hindsight. I priced my services so low because I did not want others thinking I was charging too much and ultimately lose their business. What I gained was little to no money for all the time I was putting in and clients who were not necessarily serious or ready to do business. What I gained was plenty of headaches! And I was no richer for it. This led to burnout, frustration, and second-guessing my desire to have my own business.

My advice is to take your time and be patient with yourself. Run the race that is yours. If you look to the left or the right, let it be for inspiration and not comparison. You are unique, and God's plan for your life will look completely different from someone else's. Work on yourself often, but with compassion. The better you are as an individual, the better your business will be as a company.

I no longer take on clients or work with someone I do not want to work with or do something I do not want to do.

That alone has proven to be one of the best ways to care for myself as an entrepreneur. I think a lot of entrepreneurs feel this obligation to serve those who seek us out. I know I did. I have learned that just as stores, restaurants, and other major businesses have the right to refuse service, so do I. Some clients/customers are just not worth the time and mental anguish. In addition to that simple principle, I work out, pamper myself, and am constantly aware of my health. I do the things I enjoy and that bring me joy.

I am a "stop and smell the roses" kind of woman. I am a wife and have four children. I maintain balance by giving my time and energy to the parts of my life that matter. While my business is my passion and its success matters a lot to me, it is not more important to me than the quality of life or my family. It is all about priority. As entrepreneurs, we must figure out what is important and in what order, then do that. Work hard and then make time to enjoy the fruits of your labor. I imagine one of the main benefits of being an entrepreneur is to have more control and enjoyment of our lives. We should absolutely take advantage of that benefit.

Where am I now?

I am in the rebuilding phase in my business. Somewhere along the line I forgot the reason I started in the first place. I had to slow down and reevaluate. What parts of my business did I no longer enjoy? What jobs were I taking only because I needed the money? How can I serve my client in a more holistic way? Tearing every thing down allowed me to actually see where I had gone wrong, what I actually wanted to do in my company, and how I can better show up for the people I wanted to serve. Rebuilding has been rewarding. I believe my present and future clients will benefit more now from utilizing my services.

My greatest joy on this journey has been connecting with my clients. In order for me to service them, they have to tell me their story. I love hearing how they overcame some of the greatest obstacles they have had to face. To hear how proud these women were of themselves, and to also be able to share similar experiences with them, has absolutely been my greatest joy. It makes the late nights and early mornings worth every minute.

Michele is taking advantage of the power of three words. Until I heard her explanation, I never looked at the three words as a collective for my entrepreneurial toolbox, I will now! Here is her experience.

CHAPTER 14

The power of three words:
YET, AND, BUT

I eliminate the frustrations, anxieties, and challenges tweens, teens and their families face daily at home and school. I empower them with practical tools and strategies to build their confidence, emotional intelligence, and mindset; enabling them to construct their own path to success in school and life.

~ Michele Johnson

I would have started my entrepreneurial journey a long time ago if I would have trusted my gifts, talents, and abilities. Education is about serving, and I can serve and create a legacy for my family. I did become an entrepreneur about a year ago. MJohnson Motivates was birthed from several personal pivots. Throughout the last six years, I have had to pivot multiple times from the career I built over the last 30 years as an educator.

I began as a classroom teacher in special education, and over a 30 year + period, my career includes a facilitator for professional learning for teachers, National Board-Certified Teacher for Middle School, a school administrator, and a chief academic officer. I built a career doing something I love. I have known my purpose for my life since I was six years old. I knew without a doubt at age six I wanted to be a teacher. I pursued my passion and have always been fulfilled as an educator. Now I have to be honest, once I became a school administrator and chief academic officer, my level of stress and fulfillment began to wane.

Twenty-five years in the classroom allowed me to hone my skills, I was an effective classroom teacher and a popular trainer for other educators. I was convinced I should become a school administrator. Being in leadership was a lot, and it was overwhelming. The saying is so true, you do not know what you do not know. Until you are doing the job you do not understand how difficult the job can be. Without notice, I have had to pivot from my leadership positions a couple of times in the past few years. In 2019, there was a leadership change, and I was released from my last formal leadership position. This was a challenging space for me. I spent hours and hours submitting applications for jobs outside of the norm of a school administrator. Since I love coaching teachers and helping people grow, I applied for jobs in those areas and for the most part, I avoided jobs that would require me to lead a school or an organization in any way. Okay, so I did a few of those, but for the most part, avoided them. But I submitted application after application. Initially, I got interviews, even made it to the third or fourth round of certain positions.

A few months before COVID hit I was in the process of interviewing for a well-known company. I had interviewed with them for four months because they have a very extensive process. I made it once again to the final round of an interview process. I was one week from a two-day interview in Atlanta, then the lockdown was announced. The company took a month to figure out how to interview us virtually. They did a fabulous job, and it was exhausting. We literally spent about six hours for two days interviewing individually, presenting, answering questions with teams or group interview sessions. And so, again, I did not think much of it, it was COVID. This is what was going on everywhere, and we were told they would let us know, they were not sure what this was going to look like because of COVID, they were not sure of the contracts because of COVID, and we just had to wait. While waiting, I was asked several times by friends to help them figure out how to work from home while teaching their children.

Fortunately, I have been encouraged to go into business. The most I have had to deal with, as it pertains to negative comments, is "Why have you stopped looking for jobs?", "Can't you get a job back in the classroom or as a principal again?" I was compelled to let people know that God is guiding this process and I am following the Holy Spirit. He led me into this business and entrepreneur world, and I am going to trust Him. He did not give me a job before I entered it and has not given me one since. He has given me this business and continues to show me how to grow it.

So, I began to think about how I could help and decided to start a Facebook page to share tips and advice for organizing time, space, and resources to help parents manage becoming their child's teacher or navigating what virtual school looked like in March 2019.

What most people do not know is, I was not thinking of this as a business. Friends began to encourage me to start my own business using my knowledge and skills. I had recently become a certified engagement strategist to teachers as an Independent Consultant and decided to use this certification to start my business virtually. Funny, my first thought for a business was not how I was using my skills and experience to help parents. I filled out my paperwork and was approved for my LLC., but I did not know anything about being an entrepreneur. I have been around entrepreneurs, and I have been exposed to some of the mindsets and philosophies of what entrepreneurship looks like. I supported a former spouse on his entrepreneurship journey, but I did not know anything about having my own business. Of course, since I am an educator and a learner, I started learning as much as I could. I spent hours daily during the summer attending free webinars and during COVID there were tons of them on why, how you should be an entrepreneur, or what it looks like. This was the start of how I began to feel invisible from the inside, in my own personal mindset. I was dealing with the rejection of not being able to take all my experience as a career educator and get hired before COVID.

So, I started to shrink, to become invisible. My self-confidence was shaken, and I began to shrink from all that rejection. I also unconsciously chose to become invisible because I did not think I understood or knew enough about how to be in business, how to be an entrepreneur. I had to sit back and think about my mindset concerning money. What is my mindset about abundance? What is my mindset about my own personal beliefs, about what I can and cannot do? How do I show up as myself in this space? The things I said to my students all my career like: You are an amazing person who has everything inside of you to do amazing things. You have such great potential; I want you to tap in that potential. I want you to not give up. I want you to persevere. You can be resilient. These were not things I was saying to myself yet was still passionate about ensuring every child had this mindset.

During all the webinars and workshops, you hear, find your niche, what do you love doing, what is the need in the marketplace for what you love to do? As much as I love coaching and growing educators, deep inside I knew what to do. My work with the tween and teen population throughout my career, the advice I shared with friends and family when they were tweens and teens helped with the struggle they experienced during middle and high school with organization, time management, goal setting, and having a positive mindset was my niche. These skills were needed during the pandemic and even more so once it was clear most students and families would continue to work from home as the next school year started.

Despite all the experience I have as an educator and

school administrator who worked primarily with tweens and teens, I learned I really needed to work on my own mindset. I have mentored and coached students I worked with personally over my career. I have a wealth of knowledge and experience, but even after identifying this as my niche, I learned a popular term and mindset felt by new entrepreneurs, "imposter syndrome". I began to struggle with imposter syndrome and said things to myself like, "you are not qualified to have a coaching business, what makes you think you can make a living doing this?" I also struggled with things like how do I show up, how do I find my voice again? I realized all my insecurities were causing me to hide on purpose, to spend all my time learning about business instead of taking a risk and just going out there and doing something, putting into action what I was learning, not to be afraid to "fail".

This still makes me shake my head. I do not believe failure is bad, I tell students all the time, failure is not a bad word, it is ok to try and make mistakes, you learn from these and become better at what you do. Yet I was afraid, I was insecure and began hiding on purpose. Why? Normally I am easily able to put what I learn into practice. I can take a lot of information from different sources and put it together and share it so everyone can understand it. This is one of my gifts, one of my talents. I have always been able to teach others what I learned. Why can't I do this for myself in this new space? Why can't I put the pieces together and be productive and profitable as an entrepreneur? I feel so insecure I am purposely hiding because I cannot do what I am normally good at, breaking down complex things, understanding them, and giving it back in a way anyone can understand and learn it. But I was personally struggling with how to take all this new information, something I am not comfortable with learning, and put all those pieces together so that I could create this successful business. I was learning to be an entrepreneur and it was uncomfortable, I was frustrated, overwhelmed, and telling myself all the wrong things. I became more and more invisible, I became quiet, and I lost my voice. I realized I needed to work on my mental health and deal with the rejection that I was feeling, with my own insecurities including imposter syndrome. I needed to rewire my brain and get to a place where I no longer felt I was not good enough to do this business, where my mindset and my personal affirmations, and my understanding of what it looked like to be an entrepreneur could shift into a positive place.

I had to go deep inside myself, know who I was and understand who I was from a deeper internal place. I had to remind myself of my values, of how I want to show up as my true self in business, and what that should look like so I would not be invisible. How was I going to find my voice again?

My business was birthed during the pandemic. I believe we have all been affected emotionally in so many areas by the pandemic. I see it in the teens I coach. During the pandemic, I developed the practices I needed to maintain the peace and joy in my life. I have learned several practices to help with my mental health. They include mindfulness, breathing, meditation, affirmations, exercise, yoga, and living in the present.

What I would share with other entrepreneurs is the power of three words: YET, AND, BUT; how to choose to show up for yourself and your business. Allow yourself these three words. Know this is a major part of the mindset to get you through the challenging times you will have as an entrepreneur. These words allow you to show up for yourself every day and live in your purpose.

Here is what I realized and what I remembered about who I am: I know I am kind. I know I am a hard worker, and I will not quit on myself. These small (only three letters) but mighty words helped me focus on my purpose, my mindset and show up with my voice loud and clear.

YET - Realizing I can live on purpose, walking in my purpose reminded me I can say, my business is not there YET. I had to keep saying, it is ok If I have not reached my goals

YET, it is ok if I do not know how to do everything, YET. It is ok If everything is not clear YET. When I feel like my wheels are spinning and I am going in circles, I just have not figured it all out YET. Keep saying I am not there YET. YET reminds me it is still possible, do not give up, you are going to get there, and you can do it.

AND - During this entrepreneur journey, I have had several emotions at the same time. I reminded myself it is okay to feel two emotions at one time and I am allowed to do just that. Let me break that down a little bit more. On any given day I feel like being an entrepreneur is hard AND I can do it. I can say this is overwhelming AND I can break it down into smaller pieces so I can manage it. I have learned to say to myself, I am struggling with this aspect of my business AND it is ok to ask for help.

BUT- BUT allows me to give myself grace. BUT lets me focus on not being a perfectionist, I am a recovering perfectionist. So, I have shifted to saying to myself things like, I did not get everything I wanted to do finished today, BUT tomorrow I can start again. I did not quite understand this, BUT there is more time for me to learn it. I am not making the money YET, AND I do not like it, BUT it will change. (All three in one sentence are so powerful.)

YET, AND BUT allow me to show up for myself with the right mindset. YET, AND, BUT allow me to give myself permission to grow as an entrepreneur. YET, AND BUT keeps me moving forward and not stuck. YET, AND, BUT keeps me in harmony and at peace mentally and emotionally. YET, AND, BUT help me use my strategies, tools, and practices to stay stable emotionally and mentally- mindfulness, yoga, breathing, and focusing on the present moment. I do not have to be invisible; I choose to show up for myself and allow my voice to be heard. There are tweens, teens, and families who need me, I can operate fully in my purpose, I can leave a legacy for my family and every family I touch. I realize there is no such thing as balance. I just want harmony and peace with myself. So, I am learning daily what that looks like as an entrepreneur. I have a very structured and disciplined nature. I have learned to be flexible with my schedule, what my day will look like. Some days are easier than others. But I realize I value peace, peace of mind, and spirit more than I value balance.

Where am I now?

I continue to build my parent and teen coaching offerings. My greatest joy is the success and progress of my clients as well as finally developing the systems I need to work productively in my business.

CHAPTER 15

Understanding the Market

All the business development coaches, mentors, books, etc. have encouraged us to understand the market and the many facets it encompasses. What does it truly mean to understand the market, the market you are working to enter? For me, that means, how many elementary schools are in the United States? How many students do I aim to support? Who do I partner with, who do I market to, and who will purchase my service? Where are they located? How much will the market pay for my offering? These are only a few questions to be researched to collect the data in an effort to understanding the market. In understanding the road ahead, I have learned that data is king, just like cash is king. Both come with an opportunity to support whatever goals you have set, but it still comes with the apprehension associated with the internal questions of, will the market hear you, or see you, or consider you, and what you have to offer? It can be discouraging but it is ok, because at that point the question becomes, is the person you are attempting to share your idea, products, goods, or services with, are they the right partner for you? The data will support and assist you in making a data-driven decision. Does your data support their dislike for what you are offering? The answer in my experience is no. Sometimes people are more shackled to not changing and making decisions based on fear, and other times these are diversionary tactics used to silence some for many reasons.

Women are a compliment for others and not a competition for anyone. Who wants to compete with a woman? Who wants to share the spotlight with a woman? Most importantly, why are they competing with women? Why are they not collaborating with the women? I would want to collaborate with anyone who can support me as I grow my business and have a proven track record. These questions are not always meant to be answered they are rhetorical in an effort to trigger understanding of who is your target market and who is not? If you are fishing for all fish you are fishing for none. You can not catch a shark with a hook that is meant to catch a catfish. Your ideal partner, clients, or friends have to be defined in an effort to have the market support you.

People buy products, people buy services, people are the market, so we need people and sometimes people do not always know what they need but they always know what they want, and they know how you make them feel. Without the people, you have no market. Plato says necessity is the mother of invention. He never once said the invention would be received without challenges. My experience is that as long as it comes from someone who is respected and of a certain status, the invention, suggestion, or solution is well received. Unfortunately, women have historically had to fight to be heard and with or without the proper status, she may still be dismissed. If everything stopped there, we would not have women who have made history in space endeavors, hair products, change in those most uncomfortable undergarments, and some of the medical contributions we are fortunate to have available to us to this day. Women are people! Women buy products. Women keep stores thriving and are only one aspect of any market.

I remember a comment that was made to a group of female leaders, the c-level employee explained to us all that in order to get our voices or suggestions heard whisper it into a man's ear, and then you will see how well it flies. Why? Why?

Why would another woman in a c-level position encourage a group of women to support the idea and premise that it is better coming from a man than from a woman? Is this not perpetuating the problem of women being silenced or considered invisible? How discouraging! Can you imagine not being recognized or identified for your idea, suggestion, or contribution and it makes millions and someone else gets the credit? Credit for your product or goods is not the point here. The point is, it should not always be who you know, it should be what you bring to the table. As long as everyone before you believes you are not their business we will not correct these concerns and our grandchildren will still be whispering their ideas in some man's ears.

It does not matter what you know. It matters how you handle the information received. Again, the only thing you can change is how you respond to the information. My response was educational to the person, but I do not think she learned from it nor changed her viewpoint. As long as she believes it is better to use the man to voice her idea and continues to encourage others to follow that course of action, women will stay invisible in that environment.

There is another misleading encouragement for entrepreneurs to follow that can be deadly. Let us meet Courtney as she explains her experiences and poses the question of sacrifice and how much is too much.

CHAPTER 16

How much is too much to sacrifice?

I created this business with the mindset of reaching back to my community and helping to prepare kids for the real future. I offer tutoring and enrichment services for all subjects. The reason or purpose behind this business is centered around the fact that I was not prepared. I went to college only to learn that I was not prepared. The Courte is where the kids get prepared, and they become ready to make things happen.

~ Courtney Giles

A little more about my why:

There are so many things that I needed to know that we were never taught. I know the feelings and anxieties that were created as a result of me not being prepared and I made a commitment to make certain that the kids I personally encounter never have the feelings of inadequacy that I felt when I walked on that campus back in 2003. It altered my self-confidence. It made me question this idea of me being smart and even question me belonging. Before going to college, I was excited about my accomplishments, but learning that I was not prepared and now looking back at the struggle, I was not ready. The goal of The Courte is to eliminate those feelings of self-doubt and support and prepare my kids. I never want them to feel the way that I felt. We know court as the place where decisions are made, but most importantly court is where things happen. So, for me, The Courte is where the kids get prepared, and they become ready to make things happen.

* * *

I wish I could say that I always knew or dreamed of becoming an entrepreneur, but I cannot. In fact, I almost feel like being an entrepreneur was forced upon me. I honestly did not feel like I had another option. The decision to start The Courte was birthed from a void that I was feeling in my life. I left for Austin, Texas in August of 2003, excited to be a freshman at the University of Texas. I had graduated with an abundance of accolades and recognition only to find out that I was not prepared at all. This was hard on my confidence and self-esteem, and I vowed to start a business that would serve as preventative measures to make sure that no one that came from my community or my background, would have such feelings. The thoughts and feelings of inadequacy were detrimental to me and would serve as the beginning phases of me questioning my very own existence.

I started The Courte as a platform for kids of Northeast Houston to have an advantage or an opportunity to seriously compete, not just in the world of academia, but successfully compete in life. I choose this business because in my mind I wanted to prevent them from feeling what I felt on that campus. I chose entrepreneurship because I imagined a place that would tutor those kids who were not where they needed to be and then for those who did not need tutoring, enrichment. Enrichment would serve as the push for the kids who needed it; the kids who would benefit from enrichment are the kids who felt smart and were able to keep up with the classroom curriculum, but somehow just were not being challenged. Whether participating in tutoring or enrichment, it would be a safe place for all, and I made it an environment where life lessons were at the forefront of every day.

I am guilty of feeling invisible as an entrepreneur. The invisibility is centered around the lack of support surrounding business. I feel like the cause and purpose of what I am doing is great and much needed, but access to the people and resources always seems to be very limited or in some cases non-existent. I honestly do not think that I know many entrepreneurs personally, not ones that I would label as successful. I personally feel like everyone is still waiting on their big break. The funding is hard, organizing the structure was a bit challenging and the invisibility comes because it seems like the success is a secret. I would ask for meetings or advice or ideas and everything was such a secret. I guess it always costs something to be around the people that had truly found success. But if I tell you that I am a struggling business owner you know that money is a hard thing, yet you charge me a fee to help me or for me to have access to you. I did not understand. I mean in my mind, people that appeared to be successful, had not always been in that situation, so I just think (in my simple mind), why not help me? You have been here before. You had to start somewhere, right? I did not get it. I felt invisible and the keys to success were also invisible or at least not accessible for me. And when I would go into a meeting or be on a call, I would keep my comments to a minimum because, in my mind, I did not measure up or feel worthy to be in certain situations.

The pandemic destroyed my business. Kids stopped going to school. Parents were staying home. There was a tremendous shift in dynamics. The shift affected the routines of the kids and what would be considered their norm. The other part affected the finances of the parents. The once valuable program I was offering went from being a priority and feeling like it was much needed to merely being optional. In the current state of the economy, parents were not looking for anything extra. Money was scarce and people honestly did not know what was truly going to happen and my program was canceled. But there was a new beginning. The rebuild.

I believe that one of the most important lessons I have learned about mindset is that anything and all things are possible. I feel as though I was raised with limitations and that most of what I was taught was just a routine that had been planted from past generations. The mindset was to just go to school, get a job, put in your time, move up in positions/rank, and then retire. This seems to have been a plan that had worked for generations and who the hell am I to come along and want to change it. The mindset that entrepreneurship has taught me is that there is no cookie-cutter approach to life or business. This journey has taught me to dream and think big and once I write those thoughts and dreams on paper, they become goals and aspirations. Once you break down those goals and aspirations and apply feasible planning and you put in the work, those same dreams and plans become reality. My journey with The Courte taught me that anything is possible.

In establishing The Courte, my biggest lesson learned is that I had to commit to treating my kids like human beings. It could not be a situation where I treated them as a number or just "dollar signs", I treated them like people. My mind would often go back to situations where I would think about how I wanted to be treated at that age and what could have been said or done differently to push me. My focus for them was exposure. I want them to be exposed to a variety of things and I wanted to remove the limitations. Many times, I wanted them to know there were options beyond the traditional goals that were mentioned. The lesson became that I set the tone for my business. What I was putting into it is definitely what I was going to get out of it.

The best advice that I could give to other entrepreneurs is not to ignore the signs. Take heed to your body and emotions and feelings. Pay attention to your body and stay on top of your mental health. Find a balance and implement it in business and life. The understanding has to be that you are no good to anyone if you are not healthy. The goal has to be for any entrepreneur to try and operate at their best. I used the word best to be openly interpreted and defined as you see fit, but my hope is that you identify a safe balance. Take time for self-care. Create clear and precise boundaries between business and personal life. Most importantly, find a way to completely log off. The downtime is utterly necessary.

Here I am 6 years into business, and I am just learning that there should be a self-care regime for myself and there is also a focus for me on mental health. I am guilty of not taking that time for myself in the beginning. I did not feel like I had time to do any of that because I was always working. I honestly felt like there was always something for me to do or that had to be done. I was still dreaming big even while living in my reality. I would be shopping and planning or printing on the weekend. Always on the move for the business, I honestly thought that was the way that things were supposed to be when you decide you want a business.

In the beginning, I was not even paying myself. I was putting everything back into my business. I did not realize what I was doing to myself. Hindsight…. I now know that the time away or the vacation, or day of relaxation is utterly needed. The mental health check of working in the realm of entrepreneurship makes you feel like there is no one else that can relate, and you often feel like you are on an island. Mentally the stress of it can be detrimental both physically and emotionally.

True Story: I put off having surgery for almost five years because I was afraid that my business would suffer if I had to be out for such a long period of time. Full disclosure, I had people in place that were perfectly capable of handling things, but the thought of me not being there was scary. For the record, when I mention needing to have surgery, I am talking of needing major surgery. I had a fibroid tumor that was growing, and my doctor was adamant in reminding me that it needed to be removed. It was growing and had become both uncomfortable and painful and I was dealing with it for the sake of my business. The center of The Courte was the kids. They did not know of a Ms. Courtney that had to be out or needed to recover. They did not know of me to be in pain…they had become comfortable, and their trust was that I would be there. One of the greatest fears with the kids is having an accident or something happening or even a situation not being handled properly. An incident or something major could practically destroy my business. I just could not take that chance, not with everything that I had sacrificed to accomplish thus far, so I sacrificed myself and my physical health. At the time, I admit this seemed like the noble thing to do. It made sense to me, and my understanding of this entrepreneur life is that you sacrifice and risk it all. Well, just to tell the full story, with COVID-19 drastically altering the day-to-day of my business, I was able to have my surgery this year. Just a double mastectomy. I am doing quite well now.

I personally do not feel like I have a balance, not based on the definition of balance. I have not done a great job at the separation and the need for life-work balance. Is there a balance? When it comes to The Courte, my mindset is that I had to be all in. That is the talk that I always heard. The talk of being tired cannot exist. You cannot get tired in being an entrepreneur and if something needs to be done, I am at the top of the list for who has to do it.

I remember times that I would attempt to delegate and assign tasks to my employees, but I would micro-manage them so much so that it would just make sense for me to carry out the task myself. The Courte was so delicate to me, it was my baby. It still is my baby, my child. I just feel like there are certain intricate details that I cannot teach others to pay attention to and adjust. There were always those specific details and I know me. Now, hindsight…. I understand the severe need for balance. The stress and worry that exists around your business seem to be never-ending. The pressure that always plays through my mind is the idea that I cannot mess this up; it was almost as if life depended on it. That pressure and stress surrounding my unrealistic strive at perfection and the desire to at the very least be deemed successful, there has to be balance. That type of pressure causes heart attacks and high blood pressure or strokes. But, in the moment it is a constant reminder that failure is not an option.

It cannot be an option. Even with everything that I have sacrificed, I still feel like I failed. I am my own worst critic and sometimes worse enemy, but I rate my journey thus far as a failure. That is kind of a twofold theory because my kids absolutely loved my program and everything that I was doing, but I was barely breaking even. I was struggling and with no balance I was neglecting me.

True story...I remember having to decide between paying my bills at my home and paying the bills at my building. It was a struggle, but in this situation, some people would argue that I neglected myself, but choosing the kids made me happy. To be even more honest, if I were put into this same situation again, I would still choose them. I remember for that week I was having to shower at my building because I was without power at home. It was one of those weeks that the business was hurt because of the weather and planned summer vacations, so the weekly attendance was low. If my parents knew that the child was going to miss a day, they would decide just to keep the child out that week. I understood in theory, but I did not know how to express what that was doing to me and the business. I had not thought ahead and implemented safeties for the weeks that I would have low attendance. I was so driven by the kids, but now that I think back and ponder how I would do things differently with these questions in mind, I would choose a different approach of having balance.

How does that fit or correlate with the willingness to sacrifice? Can you find a true state of balance when the business, my business may require sacrifice? I would listen to the parents, and I would take their financial situations to heart and my only focus would be that the child was present. I wanted the kids there. I remember one kid, I won't say her name, but her self- esteem and confidence was growing. She was learning how to love the skin she was in. I was teaching her to love all of her. Her mom came to me one day, about week 4, and said that she and this girl's dad had a falling out and he was refusing to financially support the kid therefore, she would not be coming to The Courte anymore. I remember my tears and hurt at the idea that I would never see her again and I could not deal with it. Without hesitation I told her to let her come anyway. "Don't worry about the money. "That was a phrase that I was beginning to say all too often. But I was doing what I was doing out of the love for the kids. They needed me and more importantly I needed them.

Balance you say, I was/am in need of a grief counselor I have had several miscarriages because of some other underlying health issues and my devotion to these kids helped me to deal with my losses. I say several, lol….by several I mean

7. It is an agonizing pain that no one talks about, but in my mind, I had found a way to deal with it all. It was the kids of The Courte that got me through. In the eyes of my parents, I assume that they just saw me as a young woman with a passion for kids and learning. But the reality is, I was hurting and confused about the reasons and the whys and in many cases angry. So, I guess The Courte was my balance. It was the balance that allowed me to hide my pain. Seeing those kids every day and being granted the opportunity to share in their lives saved me. Those moments would help me to dry my tears because The Courte gave me a taste of motherhood. Is that still balance? I guess that it is all a matter of perspective.

In my opinion, I did not encounter the "man's world" because I was operating in a realm that was intended for women. My business was one that I think limiting my position or potential is what kept me under the radar. The moment that I began to think outside the box is when I began to encounter this man's world. I had realized that there was definitely a passion for kids, and I was ready to move forward with this plan of reaching out and impacting the community. We had had an end of summer production and it broadcasted the success of the program and that seems to be when it was decided that the man would attempt to put me in my place.

I had some formal trainings and experience from my former employer, and I was ready to step on out on faith to execute and try it on my own. I entered into an agreement with the church where my family and I had been both faithful and active members. They had more than enough space that was not being utilized and, in my mind, I was surrounded by family and people that would definitely be interested in seeing me and the business and the community succeed.... but I was wrong.

This was my lesson in a man's world, and I was quickly taught that success was great, but the desire was control. They wanted control over the business but the creativity and the relationship with the parents, that was all me! All the ideas and the records and the bookkeeping and the creativity, it was in my mind. These were things and practices that I could not teach even if I tried. For them, it was about the money and for me it was a passion for the kids. That is why I started the business in the first place. They saw me introduce a process that was working, and their only concern was the headcount and the percentage that I was paying to the church. I was under the impression that because of the relationship that I had with chairman of the committee that this would somehow be the best working relationship. It was a question of money. The questions were always about money. It was me paying more and how could the "church" benefit more. I was there with the focus being the kids and ecstatic about the quality of programs that I was able to offer, and their focus was merely the money. That hurt me because it was a church, this was my family, and I just did not understand. I always thought that in the beginning of this journey of entrepreneurship, support of others especially family would be overwhelming, but this would soon turn bad. It was like they were prepared to support the failures and they were ready to say well at least you gave it a good shot. "You tried it…. Good for you!" But, in no way shape form or fashion were they ready to congratulate me on my success especially if there was no way that they could control me. Family? Church family? Confusing!

We had a meeting one night; it was our normal weekly meeting, and this was the night that I knew that there would be no coming back. It was storming that night. I came to the meeting from home because summer camp had ended. Just the scene of that night was gloomy, and I knew when I left that night that this would be the end of not only this partnership, but also the relationship. The man whom I would say was my godfather, would show me that it had to be his way or no way at all. The meeting included three other people one of which my godfather's daughter and formerly one of my best friends, there was a lady there whom she was the wife of my godfathers' best friend. The last lady, she was indeed the brains of the entire operation, but she was also the quietest. This woman was petite in stature, soft-spoken, and extremely supportive of me in private. But at that table that night, the only voice and opinion that barked loudly was that of one man. The conversation was about how to move forward. After seeing what was expected to be a failure become successful, the interest was to take over and be in control. The reality is that this was my business, my ideas and I was doing all the work, but because of the shared space I was being controlled by them. I was guilty of not utilizing contracts and setting certain guidelines to protect me because in my mind this was family, and I would not need all of this. I can laugh about this now, but this was all tears then. In that meeting on that night, they attempted to alter and streamline the approach with the kids. They wanted it to look and appeal to a certain audience, but this appeal would exclude the community where the business resided. I remember this man running off statistics for the community, Northeast Houston to be exact, and I was sitting there thinking that I am in that number that you speak of.

It was like I was less than or he was better than me or as if I were beneath the standard. My thoughts and opinions were not being heard and quite frankly it felt like my words did not matter. I left that meeting that night with the mind that I would never be controlled creatively, nor would I ever allow anyone to alter my dreams or desires. Other than to bury my uncle I have never step foot back into this church and quite frankly, apart from a funeral, I will never return.

As long as the success of my business resembled mediocrity, there was no real interest in the business. But then support began to look a lot like control. I did not get it and I just believe that it hurt more because of the people involved. But it made me go back and truly look at ways to protect my business, protect my creativity, but more importantly protect my peace.

Mindset and mental health are struggles that I was raised with, and it has been interesting to explore how they have transferred and carried over into my adulthood, they have carried over into entrepreneurship. Self-doubt was embedded in my mind at such a young age. I did not know that there was such a thing as believing and dreaming. I did not know it was ok to "color outside of the lines." I was instructed to go to school and get a job and work and retire and be okay with this plan. Also, I had to get out of the habit of asking questions.... being seen and not heard. When I graduated from high school in 2003, I was just expected to follow the plan. That was my mindset. Originally, I thought that this was a great plan and then I began to examine the people that I knew that were living this plan. The plan works in theory, it pays the bills and supports financial needs but there is no happiness or joy during the process. This just was not the mindset that I wanted to follow. This plan felt a lot like settling and it just was not the way that I wanted to go. The mental health in this plan was teaching contentment and being stagnant. It was not exactly a healthy choice either. Anxiety and depression would still begin to set in and mental anxiety of not living up to my potential or purpose would take over.

One of the most important lesson that I have learned as it pertains to mental health and entrepreneurship is that if you do not have a hold on them both, there will be no control of your mental health and that it can be damaging to the business. The mentality of entrepreneurship for me is that you have to be completely all in. All-in, to me, is a complete sacrifice of everything. In most cases, mental health is the first thing to be overlooked. Mental health is making sure there is a balance between me as the business owner and the business. Taking time to make sure that a regiment is still implemented to ensure that I am emotionally healthy. The impact that mental health has had on my journey is a bit scary and it would probably definitely be labeled as unhealthy.

I am guilty of putting an abundance of pressure on myself. Striving for perfection and the verbal and emotional abuse that I encounter as a result of not reaching perfection. It is a known fact that a goal of perfection is unreasonable. But this pressure causes stress and anxiety and in my case depression. I feel as though I was my worse and most harsh critic. One example that I most remember, I set a goal for what I thought my plan was to be. In my mind it was perfectly thought out and detailed oriented, but I soon learned that my way of thinking was a bit simple-minded. My plan did not take an abundance of other perspectives into consideration. My heart and mind were for the kids and not necessarily the business model that would allow my business to remain lucrative. I was making emotional decisions as it pertains to business. I strategically placed my business in the middle of Northeast Houston. It was an area that I was familiar with because it was where I went to high school. This emotional tie to the neighborhood caused me to make emotional decisions. The services that I offered were amazing, but I did not have the monetary support necessary to sustain them. Once I accepted the inevitable, I had to scale back and that took a toll on me. I began to beat myself up because I felt like a failure, I was turning kids away. I felt like I was no different than bigger entities that treated kids and registrations as walking dollar signs. I knew what they needed, but my limitation of funds did not allow me to provide. I kept the price for participation low because I thought that affordability would somehow guarantee loyalty, but I was completely wrong. I set my price at a point where I was barely clearing enough to pay for all of the inquired expense, but the kids were happy, and they were showing up…. what else really mattered? I struggled mentally with the idea of whether my parents would continue to bring the kids if I were to charge what my services were actually worth. Would the kids continue to come? Would the kids suffer? I worried about the conversations that would be had about me. Those are just a few of the many questions that weighed heavy on me; those were the things that I would sit up and worry about.

I had to learn the art of planning an organization. Planning would at least help to eliminate stress. My stress was that I would fail them. I felt like the kids were utterly in need of a role model or someone to admire and in many instances I felt unworthy. I spent so many nights in tears. I criticized and critique myself and I am not even certain of what I was using as the ruler, I just remember the cold words and thoughts that were constantly going through my mind.

My answer for the impact now is drastically different than what my answer would have been six years ago. My answer now is that I understand that being well mentally is equally as important, if not more, than the physical. The main battle that I have right now is my overthinking, the constant replaying of my failures and failed scenarios, the nurturing and feeding of self-doubt and I tend to see the good and all potential of everyone, EXCEPT FOR MYSELF. The impact you ask, I now know the peace of mind that is needed in order to think and organize and plan. I now understand the necessity of a support group of like-minded people. This journey can push you until you are empty with nothing to hold on to. I personally have experienced the beginning phases of depression. The feelings of inadequacy and emptiness still come to mind. There are those times when I absolutely want to give up, but I am still here. Is every day easy? Absolutely not. But I SHOW UP!

The one thing that I would do differently is that I would have started and developed my business longer before I jumped out on faith. If I would have still made the decision to attend college then I would have taken business classes and even marketing and maybe design classes. I would have taken the time to choose classes that would have helped me to nurture and develop my business. Financially, I would have found better uses of those school refund checks and incentives. While I spent money on jewelry and designer clothes, I could have been investing in myself and my business. When I think about the purchase of $200 tennis shoes, I think that with another $100, it could have been the money needed for a

Limited Liability Company (LLC). The ideas that I have jokingly put into the atmosphere because it did not seem feasible. I would do all of those things differently.

To be even more transparent, I was not taught financial literacy. There are so many mistakes that I have made when it comes to money and finances and credit that if I would have just had some additional information, I could have made informed decisions. Instead, by the time I finished college, my credit was ruined; there is no blame for me, but it was done. It would have been better to have known the significance of my credit and to know that my business would have to rely on my own credit in order to be established.

The last thing that I would think to do differently is that I would have taken advantage of networking opportunities. I have had a great distrust/mistrust of people. Adulthood was spent priding myself on being a loner and I was not open to the idea of making new friends or networking. I was raised not to trust people and I was confused about the criteria to be a friend. Those ideas would cause me to push people away and to look over the importance of networking. I felt as if I could honestly conquer the world by myself without the help of anyone. I went to one of the largest universities in the country and yet I left with hardly any friends. I started dealing with some of my medical journey in college and I did not know how to talk about it. Therefore, I kept most of it to myself. I mastered the idea of being "ok." My smile could be executed on command, but I did not realize the lasting impact that this would have on me emotionally. If I could do it all over again, I would talk and network and have conversations and learn all that was put before me. I was in a world that had endless possibilities, yet I limited myself to my own comfort zone.

Where am I now?

I am at a point where I have the opportunity to start over. COVID-19 while it had its ups and downs and has been a blessing and a curse, it put me at a point where I can start over! There are a lot of things that looking back at business I wish I would have done differently. I can now actually see the mistakes that I had made including how I handled my business financially. It just gave me an opportunity to start over.

Mentally I am at a point where I have been able to identify and communicate with other women that have some of the same struggles and some of the same insecurities and issues that I am having. I was ready to give up! I felt like I have sacrificed so much to be in business and I did not feel like I had anything else to give, so why keep trying?

It's kind of hard and bittersweet to think about because on one hand I fell in love with these kids and I do not know if they will ever really know that they saved my life. And then there is the idea that it just seems like it was all taken from me so swiftly, so abruptly. It is a whole New World; it was so hard to start, now I have to tackle the thought of starting over? Giving up just seems so much easier. But I am not going to.

One of the hardest questions to answer is when you see people you know and they ask you, "So, how is business going?" Or they ask, "are you still in business?" Because I was always so hard on myself and I could never find an answer that felt right and be good enough answer to the question. I never knew what to say. But then we enter the pandemic and I taught myself to mentally be OK with this the closing of my business because it was a national disaster. It felt like less of a slap or less of a failure because it was a worldwide disaster. I looked at it as a way that I could walk away and not be judged.

But then I was lucky enough to meet this group of women. I say meet but I was already very acquainted with Tabatha. These ladies had experienced the same trials that I have. It was a refreshing feeling that they were women, and they were having the same experiences.

I am proud to say that the rebirth of The Courte is in progress. I have learned a lot in my journey. I have sacrificed a lot. Greater is coming! I am excited!

CHAPTER 17

Know your Finances

Did you know according to Venture Beat when it comes to female entrepreneurs and access to start-up capital, whether it is a traditional bank loan or a venture capital round, women are at a big disadvantage when it comes to securing funds to start a business or grow a business. Despite the fact that they own 30 percent of small businesses, women are securing only 4.4 percent of total dollars in small business loans, 16 percent of conventional loans and 17 percent of SBA-backed loans. And once a woman is approved, her loans are significantly smaller than the loans approved for men. On the venture capital side, women-owned businesses get only about 7 percent of total venture fund investments. (VB Staff, 2019)

Maybe it is just their opinion, or their research until you read the 17 Women-Owned business stats you need to know, point #10 Women-founded companies in First Round Capital's portfolio outperformed companies founded by men by 63%. And point #13 Women receive just 7% of venture funds for their startups. (Shepherd, 2020) Now to add the information written by the Harvard Business Review …and let us just discuss one big shift that has more recently come to light, as figures from 2020 have been tallied: a substantial drop in venture capital funding for women-led startups. This was not just part of an overall decrease in VC funding. In 2019, 2.8% of funding went to women-led startups; in 2020, that fell to 2.3%, Crunchbase figures show. (Bittner & Lau, 2021) It seems small but understanding when it is millions they have removed from our potential money pot, it is significant.

My experience supports the information found but I was surprised at the numbers high and low. My concerns are that even though women follow the rules, we exceed the expectations and yet we still get less support, less respect, less money, and less consideration, in work and in entrepreneurship. No matter what, we still stay the course and play our game and still win regardless of the circumstances, being invisible is a superpower now.

The information I shared here is from well-respected

creditable companies and magazines that notice this trend and it is not meant to scare anyone away from starting a business, creating jobs, and supporting your communities with knowledge. It is so you know ahead of time the odds are stacked against us and in order to level the playing field we have to know what game we are playing. We can continue to play the waiting game or find another way to play. The lack of support can also spark a movement that allows us to join forces and level up together. Be a beacon for others as others are beacons for us. Create the change you want to see!

I met an innovative entrepreneur and she explained how she prepared for her business by saving money, building business credit, building personal finances, keeping both personal and business credit intact just in case you need it later. When I first heard her story I thought, wow if I would have known what was needed and how to do it, I could have done better and done that too. That was a spectacular example of when you have financial literacy you open your own doors of opportunity.

The path in which you go is governed by your history. My suggestion is to create another revenue stream, it is important to financially prepare for the long journey ahead and look for opportunities to not use outside money to support your vision. Work with funding outlets that support you and your dream or create a program you w

would support your demographic. If you ta

all of your baggage, and all the stuff you hav

think about it, process it, and apply it forward to y

you then will govern your own future. Tomorrow

promised, and your future has not been solidified, so a

your experience to shine a light of learning in an effort to create

the future from the lessons you have learned in your history.

Knowing where you come from and why you do some of the

things you do will allow you to choose to do things differently

in an effort to get a better outcome. The path forward is for you

and only you to create and establish with assistance from the

right community.

Money can be problematic for many but when you find

someone to add to your team who knows their worth and

yours too, it helps in the journey. Let us meet Inez an

awesome money lady!

…rth allows you
…s to get it done!

…ant to be a part of that
…ke the history, plus
…e learned, and
…our future,
… is not
…low

Accounts101

At Accounts101 we remain committed to earning our customers' trust and loyalty by providing superior accounting & payroll services with high quality, excellent value, integrity, and enthusiasm. We function as a team, work ethically, and focus on delivering the kind of bottom-line results that our clients expect and deserve. This ethos drives everything we do. From the two of our organizations to the bottom, everyone at Accounts101 understands the importance of putting our clients' needs above all else. We take a proactive approach to work with you throughout the year allowing you to leverage our knowledge and expertise for the continued growth and success of your business!

~Inez Bonner

I realized that I wanted to be an entrepreneur about 10 years ago. I was working for a landfill excavation firm at the time, and I was tasked with helping the company identify new revenue sources and at the same time cut their budget. I worked tons of hours and gave a presentation outlining how they could offer additional services, identifying labor costs and advertising costs. Additionally, I outlined how transitioning to full-time staff would be more cost-effective than hiring temp labor. Ultimately, the bid I submitted was overlooked in place of one that was submitted by a male co-worker whose bid was incomplete and doomed to fail. I realized that the power of my position was minimal because I had no real authority. I could offer a thousand solutions and in comparison to my male counterparts, I was going to go nowhere. I wanted to change that. I wanted to work with people who desired a change and were not going to diminish what I had to offer simply because I was a woman.

Sometimes I do feel invisible. I am a black, female, small business owner. I have been in conversations where I was a front runner to get a client and then they realized I was black and turned me down. No matter the 23 years of experience or multiple degrees and certifications I hold, I was still just a black woman. My knowledge was discredited without merit. I felt like they did not see me, they saw my color and gender.

The pandemic has not affected my mental health. It has boosted my business. A lot of new business owners needed to apply for PPP or EIDL loans. They did not have financial statements or the necessary information to do so. There has been a second wave of clients who now need to apply for forgiveness, and we have been instrumental in getting them approved in both instances.

My experience with the financial industry as it relates to banks has been rocky. As a newer business, it is incredibly difficult to get loans or assistance. I applied for a simple business credit card, and I was told I have not been in business long enough. The finance industry as it relates to other accountants has been interesting. My previous partner and many like him are focused on getting paid rather than customer service and support. I have learned that focusing on my clients' needs first got me a lot further along and the money comes second.

Most people go into business with their eyes shut. They operate and function as employees instead of owners. When you work for someone else you are responsible for a few things. You clock out at 5 pm and do not worry about anything till the next workday. When you own the company, you are responsible for everything and everyone. There is not an 8 to 5 schedule where you just walk away. You work hard, stay late, arrive early, and do what it takes to get it done. When it is your money you stop spending it wildly and start making choices that will hopefully guarantee a return and keep you solvent.

As a new business owner, I wish I knew how important it was to protect my brand. If you go through the trouble of coming up with a name and a logo, copyright it! I started my business under a different name, and it was stolen in a matter of weeks. I had a website, printed materials, and merchandise with that name and someone in California stole all of it and essentially copied my website nearly word for word. I had to start over. That brand recognition could have cost me clients and future work.

I learned at a very early age how to handle a lack of support or dismissing my capabilities. When I was 15 years old I became pregnant and my father told me that I had ruined my life, that I would be nothing and I would probably end up in the projects on welfare. He was very disappointed in my choices. I used that fuel to get my G.E.D, graduate college, buy a home, get married and have the life I wanted.

Just before I started my business I was kicking the business ideas around with my family member. I laid out what services I was going to offer and pricing when she stopped me and said no, it is a bad idea because I am too shy to talk to people, how was I going to get clients. I told her that I would figure it out. When you are in business for yourself you have to bet on yourself. I quit my job without a single client because I knew it would force me to step outside of my comfort zone and speak up.

Ultimately, I have always been a person who hates to be told I cannot accomplish something or do something. When people tell me I am not good enough, not capable, or not tough enough; I dig in my heels and I fight even harder to prove them wrong. My experiences have helped me understand how to create and build my business. Your first step is to shift from an employee mindset to an owner mindset. You have to think in terms of strategy and long-term growth and sustainability. When your clients begin paying you, do not immediately think of ways to spend the funds, put aside a living wage for yourself but leave the rest in the business. The more you have invested in the business the more it will grow. As for your mental health, take time for yourself and give yourself a break. You will not know everything when you get started, you will stumble and fall, you will see losses. The important thing is to learn from your mistakes and grow.

I rely on the advice and assurance of my business partner and my staff to keep me mentally in check. When things get crazy, I take those two minutes to reflect, regroup and recharge. When they are unavailable, I read my self-affirmations that I have posted on my computer monitor that reminds me that I am smart, beautiful, capable, strong and that I matter. I remember that God has made no mistakes where I am concerned.

When it comes to work-life balance, I work remotely so I have to be disciplined enough to maintain a schedule. I set a time to start and stop working and I stay committed to it. This allows me to walk away and be with my family and enjoy the life I have built. When I need a day off, I take it. I remind myself that I am human, and I need rest and recharging just like anyone else. I take small breaks to regroup. I set priorities to ensure that I meet my deadlines and I take it easy on myself for not checking everything off my to-do list at the end of the day.

Maintaining boundaries has allowed me to take my experiences and apply them to my business. I remember the one lesson that taught me that data is king.

Challenging situations happen and I remember, I took a sales meeting with an older gentleman who must have assumed I was a male because of our conversations via email and text. When I arrived, his demeanor changed, and I realized it was going to be a problem. When it was time to give my pitch I first reminded him of my education and years of experience as well as my track record for success doing what he needed. When I was finished, I went into the presentation details and outlined the many ways I was going to save him money, eliminate waste, and help his company reach the next level. I realized he was more focused on his dollars when it mattered, and I won the bid. This was a rocky start with a great outcome.

Now for the flip side. At the beginning of starting my business, I worked with a CPA who had just started his company. I helped him go from 1 client to 30 inside of a year. He began to get comfortable with the idea I was going to do whatever he needed and help the team. He gave a client a discount on my rate without asking me if it was okay. I had to stand my ground and demand that I would be paid what we contracted for even if it meant losing his business which at the time was my only business. He mistakenly thought his business was worth my integrity. He refused to budge as did I. We ended up parting ways and I was back to building my business from scratch. What I learned is that I need to know my worth, agreements matter and integrity is everything. I have now surpassed him in the number of quality clients.

When it comes to mental health, I have struggled with Bi-Polar disorder, anxiety, and depression. I know too well the struggles a person faces when their mind will not shut off or they have an overwhelming number of deadlines. For me, it is in those stressful situations where I thrive and excel. I have been fortunate enough to have a sounding board in my business partner. When clients get crazy or the day gets too hectic, I take two minutes and just voice my issues to my partner. That two-minute break allows me to clear the noise from my mind and refocus. It reminds me that I am capable, and I can handle all that is going on around me.

I learned that I cannot be everything to all people, sacrificing time for myself and my family was a quick way to burn out and my clients would bear the fruit of the suffering.

It is important to take those five-minute breaks, breathe and relax. Take joy in the small accomplishments and try not to punish myself for things that were out of my control. By adjusting my priorities to include myself I learned that we achieved more and our company was better off because of it.

My experience with the financial industry as it relates to banks has been rocky. As a newer business, it is incredibly difficult to get loans or assistance. I applied for a simple business credit card, and I was told I have not been in business long enough. The finance industry as it relates to other accountants has been interesting. My previous partner and many like him are focused on getting paid rather than customer service and support. I have learned that focusing on my clients' needs first got me a lot further along and the money comes second.

As a new business owner, surround yourself with a solid support system. This system cannot be comprised of "yes" people. It has to be people who are willing to be brutally honest. Having this type of system will help you navigate tricky business decisions and spiraling ideas that can distract from what you do and derail your progress. Pick a small group of services/products to sell and stick with it. You can always expand it later. Focus on one or two things you do exceptionally in the beginning. If you have too many pots on the stove at one time it is easier for something to get burned.

Where am I now?

We are in the process of expanding our client base. It has been a learning experience, navigating hiring staff while maintaining a level of professionalism and service that our clients have come to expect. We realized that we needed to sure up our infrastructure to maintain our current book of business and reach the next level. The best part of our journey has been helping people reach their potential. We offer an internship program that enables people to get into the accounting industry and most of our interns have gone on to do amazing things, largely because of our contribution. I have learned to trust complete strangers with the knowledge we provide, and it has paid in ways that cannot be measured.

Mental health nugget:

Money creates a lot of anxiety and stress. It can be reduced by eliminating this from the equation if you can. Create an additional revenue stream that will feed the primary business and removes the stress of looking for money.

CHAPTER 19

The reason why

When many of us talk about being invisible it is more than just that, it is being removed, dismissed, overlooked, disregarded for all the wrong reasons. Solutions, regardless of who initiates or brings it to your attention, should be considered instead of excluding because of fear. Fear shows up many ways and stops many in their tracks. What you want to accomplish has to be greater than the fear that feeds procrastination and it boils down to the question, what is the worst that can happen? Being part of the solution is not easier than being part of the problem, but it is needed for advancement and improvements.

There is always a reason we complete tasks, projects, or anything that impacts our lives. We work crazy jobs because we must make money to feed our families. We go to school because it is mandatory. We go to college because our parents tell us to go to school, get good grades, and find a good job. We become entrepreneurs to solve a problem we have experienced, or we have encountered a gap in the market. Sometimes it is for gain, other times it is to improve our health and well-being. Overall, it is normally driven by a desire to improve on what life has to offer.

Why we do our business keeps us moving toward our personal goals others may find fault in. I have learned, when your why is strong your hunger and motivation are still there pushing you to get up and take care of business! My why came from what I witnessed and my experiences. Have you ever watched a child attempt to share important information with an adult and the adult tells them to be quiet? What the child was trying to tell the adult was "I could not get my button undone to go to the bathroom", the result is the child is punished for peeing in their pants. What about when a child tries to tell the adult that someone is abusing them but because the adult is so busy, they do not stop to think how important is what the child is attempting to share. The bottom line for me is, children are people and what they have to say is important and impactful. Telling an adult "This is the wrong bus" should not be hard to listen to but it is. So my "Why" is because children need support and as many advocates as possible to support their growth.

In business, there are ebbs and flows and your WHY must be strong enough to keep you in the fight to navigate the rough terrain of entrepreneurship not to mention if you are experiencing being an invisible entrepreneur. When your why is stronger than their No, it will be a source of motivation when it is just you.

What is your Why? Do you have an experience that left you feeling as though you can do it better? Did you find that your pound cake was requested regularly by others and they are willing to pay you for it? Did you have to change your diet and found the items you were looking for were not available so you created them? Does it help keep you going through the crazy? My why has kept me going and has been a great motivator. Those healthy, safe smiles from the children, parents, and partners support me getting up every day, through the tears.

"Life's too short to learn from your own mistakes.

So learn from others"

Unknown

Kim helps us remember we are a work in progress. If we were set in stone with no tolerances for changes who would we be? And how would we progress? Let's peek into her experience!

CHAPTER 20

We are all a work in progress, and that's ok!

Kim Ribich Consulting

I am a work in progress. I believe work can be more than just a means to an end, it can be a means to deeper meaning. My mission is to be a catalyst and partner inspiring others to redesign, re-imagine, re-invent, and re-prioritize what makes life and work meaningful.

~ Kim Ribich

In 2012, I had my first taste of being a business owner when I started a side hustle at an antique mall. I had a booth where I gave old furniture new life and sold home decor/furnishings. I loved it! I originally chose to be an entrepreneur because I was burned out working in toxic workplace cultures and having little self-determination or autonomy. I wanted to use my voice to make a difference and be in service for the greater good (why I originally chose nonprofit), but instead, I felt stifled, boxed in, and pigeon-holed into support roles that did not allow me to grow or contribute all that I had the potential to contribute. I was frustrated and while I was making a decent living, I did not feel like I was making a difference.

I do not feel invisible as an entrepreneur, but sometimes as an introvert, I can feel "trampled" or overlooked/discounted because I am quiet or do more listening than talking. I have realized that while I am an introvert and welcome lots of alone time, I still am in need of community and connection. The pandemic affected my previous business as a conference planner by forcing me to shift quickly into learning how to produce virtual events. But, it also made me realize that conference planning is not my true life's work. It almost gave me permission to just throw everything out and start over. Because why not when everything else is in major upheaval. Change gets a bad rap, but change is rarely the enemy. It is only a beacon that shines a light on the things that need our attention.

Mindset, for me, is a daily practice. I have found that I need to devote time each day to working on my mindset. It is as critical as devoting time each day to building my business. And it is not something I can always do (or should do) alone!

When dealing with other people's opinions and sometimes negative suggestions I usually say to myself, "Well, that's their opinion. I have a choice about whether I take that on or not." Or I ask myself, "Is that really true for me?" I also seek out supportive people who have my back.

My advice for future entrepreneurs is, do not go it alone. Do not think that there is a "perfect" mindset to achieve. But do know what you are willing and not willing to subject yourself to. Not everyone should be an entrepreneur if it is going to seriously trigger mental health issues.

When it comes to self-care, every morning (with rare exceptions), I eat a healthy breakfast in silence. I then meditate, exercise and journal. Before I begin work, I read my affirmations. I absolutely protect my mornings for these self-care rituals because otherwise, I have a tendency of not putting my own needs first. If I skip a day I feel my energy gets depleted faster and it is easier to slip into a negative mindset. This is the embodiment of the phrase… "put the oxygen mask on yourself first before helping others."

Balance? Nope! There is no such thing as "balance" ha-ha! Entrepreneurship is an exercise in stretching and letting go and self-compassion. It is hard-core resilience training. I do not strive for balance… I strive for ENOUGH.

I do not pay any attention to the "man's world" ha-ha! I just do my thing and funny… I do not attract those types. If they try to enter my world, I firmly say "No, thank you."

The mind can be re-trained, but it takes vigilance and consistent effort. I am sensitive though to other things that can impact mental health - chemical imbalances, nutritional deficits, environmental factors, and genetic factors for example. It is not a matter of "mind over matter" and that can be a dangerous and unproductive thing to tell people.

Mental health and mindset are entwined. Entrepreneurship is not for the faint of heart. It is hard, lonely, often thankless work. There is no one to fall back on if it fails. This can weigh heavily - especially when the money is inconsistent, or you want to make a major change mid-stream. If anxiety and depression are already part of the profile (as they were for me), these stressors can make them even more apparent.

We are all a work in progress, and that's ok!

Where am I now?

Today, I work with clients around the country to uncover what is most important to them and help them re-design their lives and work in alignment with their core needs and values. In addition to deepening my 1:1 coaching and résumé writing practices, I am developing workshops and online content exploring what it means to be a work in progress. Hopefully, when this is published, I am on sabbatical in Santa Fe, finishing the book I have been working on for the last several years.

My biggest joy is witnessing clients unlock their potential and reconnect with their inner authority. There is so much power available to us all when we get out of our own way, get clear about what is most important, and decide to take action. The moment something clicks is the moment clients become unstoppable. It's incredible to watch! The biggest joy through my own personal journey is having connected with an incredible community of women. They refuse to be invisible and they motivate me every day to show up and lead with heart.

"Every time you state what you want or believe, you're the first to hear it. It's a message to both you and others about what you think is possible. Don't put a ceiling on yourself."

- Oprah Winfrey

Now to meet me! I have learned that every experience has a lesson and I have to be willing to learn the lesson otherwise it continues to repeat. Here is my experience to add to the lessons.

CHAPTER 21

The lesson is in the struggle, find it, learn from it, and use it!

CHILD TRANSIT SAFETY MADE SIMPLE

We help children go home the way the parents intended. No more children left on the bus or dropped off at the wrong stop. Everyone goes home on time Every time and you as the parent receives a text message. We partner to save a life, save a job, and provide peace of mind to everyone taking care of our children.

~Tabatha Barron

I knew when I was about 9 or 10 years old I needed to help people and create a place where catch 22's were not prevalent. At that age I did not realize it was entrepreneurship that I needed to embark upon, I just knew I needed to do something. I finally made the decision to start my business in 2014 when my niece was placed on the wrong school bus twice in her kindergarten school year at the age of 5. I finally figured out what I could create that would help support other people and I made the plunge.

At times I do feel invisible. I work really hard to follow the rules of engagement and when I show up and speak with intelligence, talk with the right person, and the invisibility begins. People have misled me to believe they are engaging with me as a human being and with respect, shortly after, their true intent is revealed, and it is another example of not being the right fit for them. Many of these encounters have left me scratching my head and reviewing the situation and experience for an understanding of what I need to change, resolve, and improve upon and then it hits me. Is this not the same bad behavior I experienced in a male-dominated field? Yep! So, I use it as my superpower to find the right people to created impactful and resilient partnerships. With that understanding, I work to shelve the feeling of invisibility so I can get to work. For me when I understand the root cause, I can find a way around the hurdle.

The pandemic has forced me to incorporate some self-care practices to get out of my head. I decided to begin roller skating again and to carve out time just to be quiet or have lunch or just a moment to breathe. I give myself permission to take a day to do nothing when things are not feeling as hopeful as I would like them to be. I tell myself every day "I am Enough even if they say I am not!" I also took this time to work on some of the day-to-day heavy lifting that needed to happen to improve the business but it also allowed me the space to create a huddle in an effort to create a community needed to support me in the upcoming years. The reason for the book came out of the huddle because as I was looking for something, we all found each other. Ladies to support, share accountability, improve our outlook, and be a beacon of light for others that may be working to escape the crab in a barrel process that is strongly promoted. We have created a safe space to discuss the OBGYN of finances, the marking bloopers of business, and to support the good, the bad, and the ugly without judgment only with love and kindness. We share our wins and our losses as a way to share what works and what does not. It has been empowering and impactful!

On this entrepreneurial journey, I have found that mind over matter is a LIE for me. Pushing to get to the undefined mindset everyone is talking about has been problematic for me. I realized that mindset is only limiting if I allow those limits to exist, and limitless when I recognize my strength. Mindset is a journey, not a destination, and I always have to evaluate my mindset regularly to determine the efficacy per situation. I would not drive my car for years on the same oil, why would I drive myself with the same mindset for years. My vision has not changed but my perspective and mindset may have to in order for my learning to continue, my growth to happen, and my awareness to improve. I do get angry when people tell me to change my mindset because I disagree with their viewpoint. Mindset is personal and different for everyone, and we must do what is best for ourselves. It is okay to differ in opinions of mindset, but it is never ok to attempt to force a mindset change to meet someone else's personal agenda.

I have been met with many negative comments for various reasons from sales, marketing, investment meetings, and technology gurus. I found negative comments are common when doing things differently from others. It is also good to note that I do not have young children so they cannot be the motivation for this, I am doing it because the children count, PERIOD! I remember one time when I was invited to an event to meet investors, I was not sure if it was the greatest idea, but I went and heard some great information and then I was introduced to the man that I was invited to meet. When I stood in line and then I finally got my turn to speak with him,

I did my 10-second pitch only for him to tell me, that is not a real problem, it is an inconvenience go find something else to solve. My next question to him was, "so it is inconvenient to have a child get on the wrong childcare bus and go to a center that is different from the one you paid for your child to attend all without your permission? Do you believe it is ok for a stranger to leave with a child that does not belong to the family? That's inconvenient?" His answer was YES, it is still an inconvenience. After I closed my mouth in disbelief at what he said and how he said it, I was pretty irritated and learned that not everyone is meant to go for the ride, and I needed to be selective about who I spoke with and who I look to for support. Although he was rude about what he said and how he said it, he helped me remove his demographic and gender from my target market. I learned that some men are not my target marketing because of how they view nurturing, protecting, and communicating with our young impressionable people so I cannot expect them to find the value in safety, growth, and independence, all of which I am working to provide. I have been told they care more about the bottom line and not the feelings attached. It was a hard pill to swallow but I did because the market spoke to me with that message. I could choose to continue speaking with them or move on and find the right partner. Thanks for the lesson, I will look for the right partner.

When I speak with other entrepreneurs or when I am asked advice about entrepreneurship I explain two things, 1. your why has to be strong enough to withstand the ebbs and flows of the journey. It is a tough journey where plans, marketing plans, business plans, sales plans, and social media plans may change and force you to adapt to the wake change leaves. When your why is strong, the changes will not take you out. My why is very strong because it is not about me it is about the voice of the child that does not get heard if I stop advocating for them. 2. Improve your financial situation, I wish I would have positioned myself in a better financial situation to begin this process, for example learning to setup savings, business credit, business accounts, and understand monthly overhead are just a few things that are important to the financial needs or preventable strain entrepreneurship brings. Also, I encourage creating another form of revenue that will support the business as you strategically grow.

I am really bad at self-care. I have a hard time believing that I am not being selfish by taking care of myself first. With so much going on I have learned it is better to put my own oxygen mask on first, so I have set aside time to roller skate daily. I can only think of one thing while I am roller skating, how not to fall, LOL. I drink a lot of water and remind myself that I am enough, and I am okay just the way I am. I do not need to be fixed or compared to another because two gems will never be identical.

When it comes to entrepreneurship, maintaining balance is extremely challenging. From my standpoint, there is no balance, yet. We work until and then we push a little further to meet the goals and commitments previously outlined for ourselves. I believe the balance occurs once we have achieved a level of success that allows for at least our basic needs to be met. Balance in life is hard to maintain in general but it is definitely important to set boundaries and expectations for myself and others in order to understand the type of controllable balance needed for a healthy existence. I have established what success looks like for me and I will work towards that goal and then when I accomplish the pre-determined goal I have set, the process will usher me into the work-life balance I desire for myself.

Navigating challenging situations has not stopped after I stopped working for others. My experience with higher ranking decision-makers has been destructive toward me personally and professionally and that was not what I expected from educational leaders or leaders, period. I remember one school district had a few parents very upset about the fact their children had been placed on the wrong school bus multiple times within the same school year and when the parents asked the school and the district for support to ease their concern, they were met with a laundry list of reasons why the product we offer was not an option. What was weird was the principal where one of the incidents occurred expressed an interest in adopting the program. So, I went to the board meeting with the parent, and they spoke first and let the school board know why she was there and then I proceeded to explain the stats and how we could assist in minimizing and eliminating these kinds of incidents they consistently experience. I expressed the desire to form a partnership with them and the families they support and all those who are interested in the opportunity to improve a manual process already in place. What he did next was by far the most destructive thing I thought an educator would do. He attempted to pit two parents against one another. He lied to the parents about the company and our proposal and then told them to place a cellphone in his backpack so then they could track their child all the time. The superintendent did not acknowledge, apologize, or provide any comfort, or show empathy for the families or the children. That is hard to witness because these are the people we let educate, protect, and care for our children in our absence. This changed my approach and helped me to narrow my target market.

To have someone in a higher position remove the option to answer the request of parents was extremely surprising, what made it worse was the extend of the lies being told and the total disregard of the anxiety the child had been experiencing since the incident. WOW! What do you do with that? I recognized that again he was not my target audience because he presented the same way the investor did and so at that point, I realized some things should not be kept a secret, so when I am asked by parents in the district about joining their district I just inform them we cannot offer our services as their district is not open to the improvements. I just allow this to be an example of, not everyone is meant to go on the ride, and I look for the next partner that understands and values the product and what it offers to them. Peace of mind for all involved in the child's day.

A couple of things to note.

- *A cell phone in the backpack does not resolve the anxiety of the child after you place them on the wrong school bus, and they must sit quietly on the ride while personally dealing with situational anxiety because they have been ignored or told to be silent. The adult knows more than them. Meanwhile, the child expressed concern and not allowed to speak.*
- *The fact they do not accept responsibility for the uncomfortable position they put the families in is nothing but an example of the lack of teamwork and community we*

as parents and taxpayers are expecting from our leaders educating our children.

Acknowledgment is where the obligation to do something begins. I under- stand this is my experience, and it just reminds me that some secrets are not meant to be kept and my why will help me find the right school partners to help support the children and families they education. We all need to nurture these children, as they are all our future. I was truly hurt by the experience, and it caused me to pause my efforts for a brief moment, I had never experienced the level of unnecessary hatred from a person in leadership for no reason until him. His horrible email, and the lack of concern I felt existed in education was surprising off the charts, and then I spoke with my support team, and they helped me to remember my why, and I tell myself daily I was built for this, he is not the only person on the planet so go and find the others. It is hard and yes I slide back but I still keep pushing.

I always remind myself; change is not easy, no one likes hearing their current solution is not yielding the favorable results they are expecting. Is there really a problem to be solved, no, there is just an opportunity to improve and support an already existing one. For those reasons, I look for those who understand the importance of child safety and they support the foundation we have created in an effort to pay it forward.

I have also learned that other entrepreneurs can be just as mean and without compassion because I had an experience with a fellow female entrepreneur, and it left me cracked but not broken. I was referred to her for support and when I spoke with her, support is not what I received. She pretty much encouraged me to close the business and work on myself, and the words she used without understanding why I was contacting her, left me in my head all day. I was looking for support, understanding, and a different viewpoint from someone who was on a similar journey. Being able to learn from someone else experience, for me, is a great way to learn. She was not a good teacher nor was she a good example of community or squad. After all the dust settled I ended up helping her with a problem she had but she had no sense of responsibility for the damage she may have caused someone else walking the challenging road as an entrepreneur. To this day, I make sure to listen or at least pay attention to the intuition that I call my tuning fork and when it tells me, it is not a good idea, I stop. This experience with her forced me to remember that crabs in a barrel exist in places I did not expect and with people of all success levels. It is common for those behaviors to be rewarded and encouraged. I limit my interaction with people that trigger a heightened response, and

I take the lesson and apply the filter to not allow any unwanted community members. It is important to protect your peace, mental health, and mindset with the boundaries that will support me in my journey.

When I think about mental health and mindset, I think about protecting myself from the outside elements because the right mindset will support your mental health. I know where I am, I know where I want to go, and I am aware this is where mindset begins. Where the two intersects or collides can determine the outcome but does not stand alone in not reaching my personal goals. I am the only one that can set my mindset to a fixed mindset, one that does not allow for much growth, or a growth mindset, one that allows for me to learn from others. I chose a growth mindset because I am a very inquisitive person and that is where growth can be found. From there I can protect my mental health based on the core values that support the mindset needed to support others and thrive.

I have learned that community means everything when it comes to my personal mental health while traveling the highway of entrepreneurship. When they say iron sharpens iron, they mean it! Inside the right community, I can thrive, and my mental health challenges seem to lessen. When I am in a community that is not conducive to my personal goals, I notice that I have more challenges and begin to question my decisions and vision. For those reasons, I choose to surround myself with a community that embraces me for who I am and who accepts and uplifts me instead of criticizing and catastrophizing my journey. It is very important to have the right support to protect and insulate yourself from depression, anxiety, and various challenges along the way. Our why must be stronger and bigger than the worse thing they will say about you and me. Because as I have learned they are watching even when you do not think they are, they are watching to see if you truly believed in your dream, vision, or path yourself. I use it as additional fuel for my journey and thank you for the indirect support.

Being invisible is not what the definition suggests, it is bigger than that. It is when you have knowledge and skills to bring to the table and the decision- makers say, your opinion is not wanted. It is when you have done the work, have gotten the education, have the experience, and met the goal only for your efforts to be dismissed and minimized. Women historically are silent cheerleaders with no voice and that is unfortunate because invisibility is one of our superpowers because you never see us coming and what you get far exceed the overall expectations.

Where am I now?

Education took a hit, but I am still working towards my goal to support 10M children with the right education leaders as partners. I have added a fundraising aspect with the idea to put money into the schools they can use as a way to financially five back.

Paying it forward with no expectations.

CHAPTER 22

How it will all continue

There is no ONE answer for the journey you are on. This is an opportunity to use your individual and critical thinking skills to make the best decision for you. Some of us have been told during our journey that we must sacrifice, sacrifice, sacrifice even if it means eating from the dollar menu for years or sleeping on a friend's couch until they put you out. Others have been told to change how we do anything or everything because it is not conducive to their feelings for you or me. Others have had great experiences and support that we would all love to have in our journey. The point is, we are in multiple industries, and we contribute to the larger picture all the time, our experiences are just that, our experiences. Our lessons can be used as a guide for you on your journey and remember you are not alone with how you feel. Take from our experiences the things that work, leave behind those things that do not serve you, and share your experiences with others because there is enough for everyone to have a piece of many pies. The more we share, the more we grow together, the more we challenge the status quo and the concept that women cannot do it together.

During the preparation of this book, I received a lot of different opinions and in some cases negative limiting beliefs. That was weird because, after you told me I have limiting beliefs you then inject your limiting beliefs into my experience. What is the end game? Is it because you have not accomplished your goals YET, that you believe that I can never accomplish mine? That is a mindset of scarcity and part of the interruption that is injected to slow down those who are challenging the system created to exclude and eliminate whoever does not fit the goals or the idea of who they may want in leadership. Is the reason you are suggesting I change my mindset, perception, strategy, or whatever because you benefit from the broken system in place, and you are not interested in changing yourself? This is problematic because history teaches us the lessons for the future and the lack of willingness to see another perspective gives us a limited vision of the larger picture. I have never been against learning or listening to another possibility it is only when I start to not recognize myself or my vision in the changes that I stop. What about you?

With all of the experiences in the book, I hope you are able to understand how you participate, contribute, perpetuate, or ignore the stigma of women. With all of the experiences in the book my hope is that someone's story will resonate enough with you that you find the answer to that nagging question, or it lights a way for you to grow, or you find the inspiration in yourself to go and be the greatest version of yourself. My ask is before you begin to blame the woman whose experience is different from yours, please ask yourself a question, is it possible that her experience can be different from yours? Is it possible that her experience is an opportunity to re-write the rules enough to include her or open a door she does not have access to alone? Victim blaming, regardless of where it is done, is not acceptance or acknowledgment of her. Our ultimate goal in life is to build a legacy for our families, to change the narration of our individual stories, and to leave the world a little better than we found it. This is done by uplifting, encouraging, supporting, and celebrating our differences. Now that we know, we are now obligated to do something. We are waiting for you.

I was speaking with a few different ladies and shared my experience. I have a strong personality, most people who know me have confirmed this fact. The one thing people do not see is that when I walk into a room with other leaders, I will shrink myself, hide my knowledge, and move into the shadows of the room because I do not want to be called aggressive, rude, accused of wasting time, or any other comment said that makes me think I am unwanted there. Writing this book helped me see how I am self-inflicting invisibility, and I will make a more conscious effort not to do it anymore. For those who say, well that was your issue not to be confused with my experience. I always remember I am my sister's keeper! The wake she leaves is additional hurdles I must overcome. It may not be now, but no one is immune to the possibilities of later.

It did not start with me, and it will not end with me. We could all decide to show up authentically ourselves and challenge a broken thought process, system, and the game we are all being forced to play with a limited understanding of the rules that are always changing. She who controls the narrative controls the story. No one sets the rules of engagement but you. If we do not like the rules, change them, build different bridges to our dream, and use the tenacity we were created with to push us forward. We see people doing it every day.

Since writing my story I have been told by the men in the room to change my mindset, to reduce myself because the men have insecurities that I highlight and expose, and I have also been told that I can be an authority in my industry. The comments run the gamut. Here is what I will say. I have already gone within before I we begin to speak and do it regularly to ensure I am not blocking my lesson. Here is my challenge to the men with those varying comments, please look at your own perspective and evaluate your mindset first, and that would include the intent behind your statements and comments. Keep in mind while you are telling me, pointing with one finger, to change my mindset, there are three fingers pointing back at you to do it three times more. Ask yourself, what do you have to gain by me changing my mindset to what is conducive for you? Is there a guarantee with the change you are suggesting for me? For those men with insecurities, do your work! If the expectations for us is to be ready, to be together, to be prepared, and for our insecurities and feelings to be left in the umbrella stand at the front door, you may want to check yours there too. Please do not ask us to do what you cannot do yourself because if you cannot do it, why should we? Our strength is in the humanity we all possess.

Ladies, please do your work! We spend a lot of time taking care of everyone else needs that sometimes there is not enough time to take care of ourselves. We are spectacular people with amazing gifts that many can benefit from but if we do not take care of our mental health we will not have longevity in our dream. No one can push you to create, seek help, and support but I can tell you from personal experience, if you do not want to lose control over your direction, you better do something. Mental health is our oxygen in life and our saving grace, manage it for yourself with the same tenacity you use for others.

Now that we have peeked into a small portion of the lives of various female entrepreneurs, do you have a different outlook? Our hope is you are able to see what lessons we can all learn from the contributors of this book and ones you know personally. The next time you see a small business are you going to support? The next time you notice your friends or family members trying to be entrepreneurs, are you going to think twice about how to support them? My hope with all of the stories shared, and some may be hard to read, is that you can actually reach out to one of the businesses and support them, by respecting their prices, by appreciating their abilities, by embracing a different narrative, beside a great woman can be a strong supportive man.

Sometimes some women do not call it being invisible but being marginalized, dismissed, taking over your stuff, are all different forms of invisibility and it shows up in multiple areas in our lives, whether we work for someone or we have others working for us. There are many ways invisibility is initiated, it comes from childhood, it can be perpetuated with employers, it can be self-induced, or outright being told to you by others. The only thing we can control is how we respond to it and how we use it to our benefit.

There are a lot of female entrepreneurs who find opportunities to apply their solutions to various systems and if we could just hear her out without judgment or unconscious bias, we all have the chance to be better for the experience. We recognized that some women may not feel marginalized, invisible, or dismissed but some do and at the same time we can all admit that exclusion is the best deterrent to avoid competition. It is challenging for women to take certain higher-ranking positions but there are some that do. There are some well-known female entrepreneurs who have shown what capabilities we possess, and we need more.

At the end of the day, we are remarkable, we are not broken, and we come with compassion, a different vantage point, and a customizable way to look at opportunities for enhancements and not problems to be solved. We are the market and we are moms, sisters, daughters, aunts, grandmothers, and a great asset to the right team. Do not sleep on us, because you have given us the best superpower to have,

Invisibility. Why do I say that? Because as long as you see us as invisible, you will never see us coming.

The invisible entrepreneur is also a powerful one.

Reach one, Teach one

No country can ever truly flourish
if it stifles the potential of its women
and deprives itself of the contributions of half of its citizens.
Michelle Obama

Appendix 1

Here is a partial list of questions used to compile the stories in this book. Each story was inspired and completed because of these questions and is in their own words.

- When did you know you wanted to be an entrepreneur? & Why did you choose to be an entrepreneur?
- What is the most powerful lesson you have learned about mental health and entrepreneurship? And what impact has it had on your journey?
- What is the most important lesson have you learned about mindset and entrepreneurship? Please provide an example.
- What are your thoughts about mindset and mental health?
- Do you feel invisible as an entrepreneur? Why or Why Not?
- What is your self-care regime to keep your mental health in check as an entrepreneur?
- Provide two examples of how you were able to navigate a challenging situation in a "man's world" as an entrepreneur.
- How do you maintain balance, if at all?

- How has the pandemic affected your mental health and your business?
- What advice would you give other entrepreneurs when it comes to mindset and mental health?
- What is the one thing that if you knew then what you know now, you would do differently?

References

Alice Broster, C. (2020, October 28). *Self-Employed Women Are At A Higher Risk Of Having Poor Mental Health, According To Study.* Retrieved from https://www.forbes.com/sites/alicebroster/2020/10/28/self-employed-women-are-at-a-higher-risk-of-having-poor-mental-health-according-to-study/?sh=47c55c4e17f6

American Foundation for Suicide Prevention. (2021). Retrieved from https://afsp.donordrive.com/index.cfm?fuseaction=cms.page&id=1226&eventID=7357

Anna Pitts, G. R. (2013, April 8). *You Only Have 7 Seconds To Make A Strong First Impression.* Retrieved from https://www.businessinsider.com/only-7-seconds-to-make-first-impression-2013-4

Bittner, A., & Lau, B. (2021, 02 25). Retrieved from Harvard Business Review: https://hbr.org/2021/02/women-led-startups-received-just-2-3-of-vc-funding-in-2020

Dan Murray-Serter, F. C. (2020, October 4). *Why Entrepreneurs Need To Talk About Their Mental Health.* Retrieved from Forbes: https://www.forbes.com/sites/danmurrayserter/2020/10/04/why-entrepreneurs-need-to-talk-about-their-mental-health/?sh=dd7765a37d02

Doane, B. (2018, 06 20). *Forbes.com.* Retrieved from https://www.forbes.com/sites/yec/2018/06/20/5-mental-health-rules-for-entrepreneurs/?sh=25b6f8837784

Koṫlawī, A. Y. (n.d.). *Akhlāq-uṣ-Ṣāliḥīn.* Karachi, Pakistan: Maktaba-tul-Madīnaĥ.

Mental Health America. (2020). Retrieved from
    https://mhanational.org/issues/2020/mental-health-america-
    prevalence-data

Merriam-Webster. (n.d.). Retrieved from https://www.merriam-
    webster.com/dictionary/

Shepherd, M. (2020, 12 16). *Fundera.* Retrieved from
    https://www.fundera.com/resources/women-owned-business-
    statistics

VB Staff. (2019, 07 17). *The rising ROI of investing in woman
    entrepreneurs.* Retrieved from Venture Beat:
    https://venturebeat.com/2019/07/17/the-rising-roi-of-investing-
    in-woman-entrepreneurs/

Additional Reference/Resource Links

- Venture Beat
  https://venturebeat.com/2019/07/17/the-rising-roi-of-investing-in-woman-entrepreneurs/
- Fundera
  https://www.fundera.com/resources/women-owned-business-statistics
- Harvard Business Review
  https://hbr.org/2021/02/women-led-startups-received-just-2-3-of-vc-funding-in-2020
- Business Insider
  https://www.businessinsider.com/only-7-seconds-to-make-first-impression-2013-4
- Forbes
  https://www.forbes.com/sites/danmurrayserter/2020/10/04/why-entrepreneurs-need-to-talk-about-their-mental-health/?sh=dd7765a37d02
- Forbes
  https://www.forbes.com/sites/alicebroster/2020/10/28/self-employed-women-are-at-a-higher-risk-of-having-poor-mental-health-according-to-study/?sh=47c55c4e17f6
- Mental Health America
  https://mhanational.org/issues/2020/mental-health-america-prevalence-data
- American Foundation for Suicide Prevention
  https://afsp.donordrive.com/index.cfm?fuseaction=cms.page&id=1226&eventID=7357

- o Research
  https://www.research.va.gov/topics/suicide.cfm
- o Centers for Disease Control and Prevention
  https://www.cdc.gov/nchs/data/databriefs/db355_tables-508.pdf
- o The Eagle
  https://theeagle.com/opinion/editorial/meghan-markle-puts-a-spotlight-on-the-epidemic-of-suicide/article_1d9eb35a-83ac-11eb-95b4-df4c6be1fa1b.html
- o The Guardian
  https://www.theguardian.com/society/2019/jun/03/mental-illness-is-there-really-a-global-epidemic
- o National Alliance on Mental Health
  https://nami.org/Home
- o National Institute of Mental Health
  https://www.nimh.nih.gov/health/statistics/suicide
- o Calmer
  https://www.thisiscalmer.com/blog/how-to-manage-mental-health-entrepreneur

Made in the USA
Columbia, SC
06 August 2021